CURIO NO. 7

READ THE CLASSICS

THE BOOKS THAT NURTURED HUMAN THOUGHT

MATTHEW DOUCET,
Editor

CIDER MILL PRESS

BOOK PUBLISHERS
KENNEBUNKPORT, MAINE

13-Digit ISBN: 978-1-60433-968-0
10-Digit ISBN: 1-60433-968-3

This book may be ordered by mail from the publisher. Please include $5.99 for postage and handling. Please support your local bookseller first!
Books published by Cider Mill Press Book Publishers are available at special
discounts for bulk purchases in the United States by corporations, institutions, and
other organizations. For more information, please contact the publisher.

Cider Mill Press Book Publishers
"Where good books are ready for press"
PO Box 454
12 Spring Street
Kennebunkport, Maine 04046
Visit us online!
www.cidermillpress.com

Typography: Rival
All vectors used under official license from Shutterstock.com.
The Metamorphosis courtesy of The Kafka Project.
All other texts courtesy of Project Gutenberg.

Printed in Singapore
1 2 3 4 5 6 7 8 9 0
First Edition

CONTENTS

INTRODUCTION

NEVER-ENDING news cycles and social media swipes and likes have narrowed human perspective to the palms of our hands and the 18 inches between us and the screens that we plant ourselves in front of day in and day out (both for work and pleasure). We memorialize the present before the moment even has time to pass. The ceaseless tides bestow breaks between swells, at least. The now, now, now of media, however, is more like a fire hose in the face, one that cannot be turned off. In such a rush of information, data, and memes and jokes gone viral there isn't a moment to orient oneself in this frenetic and ephemeral landscape.

But, with a look back through the past, the present and future can come into clearer focus if disruptive digital ad campaigns are understood within the context of the mark making of ancient cave art. Or if we try to understand contemporary alienation as it is personalized in Franz Kafka's *The Metamorphosis*, reminding readers that we can indeed control our fate, even if such a prospect feels hopeless.

And speaking of "fate," where did concepts like "free will," "fate," "reincarnation," "the natural condition," and "realism" originate? And what of the literary devices by which these concepts were shaped into words, like metaphors and parables? The excerpts found on the following pages outline the development of human thought, making clear that before the world was known as it is today, when existence was contained within a village or city-state, we have always been connected by the innate desire to know more, and this is what we have shared in common since time immemorial, no matter the height of the mountains that stood between us, or the breadth of the oceans that extended from our shores.

We will start "In the Beginning" and learn how we taught ourselves to tell stories and develop our ideas. As we move through history, think of these fragments as pieces of a mosaic that, once it is filled in, will depict a scene of critical thought that can be applied to any and all circumstances that arise today.

Let us live in the moment to our fullest by understanding how each passing second is connected to all those that have come before it, as well as all of those that will follow.

IN THE BEGINNING

HOMER
THE ILIAD

trans. Samuel Butler

The staggering accomplishments of the Ancient Greeks were, as Hegel points out, "commenced" by the plight of Achilles in The Iliad. *So ashamed were they of a society that could privilege the unwarranted status of Agamemnon over the brilliance of Achilles that they set about ensuring it never happened again. In constructing a culture where individuals were allowed to relentlessly pursue their particular genius, they ended up producing systems, philosophies, and technologies that the West is built upon.*

They found Achilles sitting by his tent and his ships, and ill-pleased he was when he beheld them. They stood fearfully and reverently before him, and never a word did they speak, but he knew them and said, "Welcome, heralds, messengers of gods and men; draw near; my quarrel is not with you but with Agamemnon who has sent you for the girl Briseis. Therefore, Patroclus, bring her and give her to them, but let them be witnesses by the blessed gods, by mortal men, and by the fierceness of Agamemnon's anger, that if ever again there be need of me to save the people from ruin, they shall seek and they shall not find. Agamemnon is mad with rage and knows not how to look before and after that the Achaeans may fight by their ships in safety."

Patroclus did as his dear comrade had bidden him. He brought Briseis from the tent and gave her over to the heralds, who took her with them to the ships of the Achaeans—and the woman was loth to go. Then Achilles went all alone by the side of the hoar sea, weeping and looking out upon the boundless waste of waters. He raised his hands in prayer to his immortal mother, "Mother," he cried, "you bore me doomed to live but for a little season; surely Jove, who thunders from Olympus, might have made that little glorious. It is not so. Agamemnon, son of Atreus, has done me dishonor, and has robbed me of my prize by force."

As he spoke he wept aloud, and his mother heard him where she was sitting in the depths of the sea hard by the old man her father. Forthwith she rose as it were a grey mist out of the waves, sat down before him as he stood weeping, caressed him with her hand, and said, "My son, why are you weeping? What is it that grieves you? Keep it not from me, but tell me, that we may know it together."

Achilles drew a deep sigh and said, "You know it; why tell you what you know well already? We went to Thebe the strong city of Eetion, sacked it, and brought hither the spoil. The sons of the Achaeans shared it duly among themselves, and chose lovely Chryseis as the meed of Agamemnon; but Chryses, priest of Apollo, came to the ships of the Achaeans to free his daughter, and brought with him a great ransom: moreover he bore in his hand the sceptre of Apollo, wreathed with a suppliant's wreath, and he besought the Achaeans, but most of all the two sons of Atreus who were their chiefs.

"On this the rest of the Achaeans with one voice were for respecting the priest and taking the ransom that he offered; but not so Agamemnon, who spoke fiercely to him and sent him roughly away. So he went back in anger, and Apollo, who loved him dearly, heard his prayer. Then the god sent a deadly dart upon the Argives, and the people died thick on one another, for the arrows went everywhither among the wide host of the Achaeans. At last a seer in the fulness of his knowledge declared to us the oracles of Apollo, and I was myself first to say that we should appease him. Whereon the son of Atreus rose in anger, and threatened that which he has since done. The Achaeans are now taking the girl in a ship to Chryse, and sending gifts of sacrifice to the god; but the heralds have just taken from my tent the daughter of Briseus, whom the Achaeans had awarded to myself.

"Help your brave son, therefore, if you are able. Go to Olympus, and if you have ever done him service in word or deed, implore the aid of Jove. Ofttimes in my father's house have I heard you glory in that you alone of the immortals saved the son of Saturn from ruin, when the others, with Juno, Neptune, and Pallas Minerva would have put him in bonds. It was you, goddess, who delivered him by calling to Olympus the hundred-handed monster whom gods call Briareus, but men Aegaeon, for he is stronger even than his father; when therefore he took his seat all-glorious beside the son of Saturn, the other gods were afraid, and did not bind him. Go, then, to him, remind him of all this, clasp his knees, and bid him give succor to the Trojans. Let the Achaeans be hemmed in at the sterns of their ships, and perish on the seashore, that they may reap what joy they may of their king, and that Agamemnon may rue his blindness in offering insult to the foremost of the Achaeans."

Thetis wept and answered, "My son, woe is me that I should have borne or suckled you. Would indeed that you had lived your span free from all sorrow at your ships, for it is all too brief; alas, that you should be at once short of life and long of sorrow above your peers: woe, therefore, was the hour in which I bore you; nevertheless I will go to the snowy heights of Olympus, and tell this tale to Jove, if he will hear our prayer: meanwhile stay where you are with your ships, nurse your anger against the Achaeans, and hold aloof from fight. For Jove went yesterday to Oceanus, to a feast among the Ethiopians, and the other gods went with him. He will return to Olympus twelve days hence; I will then go to his mansion paved with bronze and will beseech him; nor do I doubt that I shall be able to persuade him."

On this she left him, still furious at the loss of her that had been taken from him. Meanwhile Ulysses reached Chryse with the hecatomb. When they had come inside the harbor they furled the sails and laid them in the ship's hold; they slackened the forestays, lowered the mast into its place, and rowed the ship to the place where they would have her lie; there they cast out their mooring-stones and made fast the hawsers. They then got out upon the sea-shore and landed the hecatomb for Apollo; Chryseis also left the ship, and Ulysses led her to the altar to deliver her into the hands of her father. "Chryses," said he, "King Agamemnon has sent me to bring you back your child, and to offer sacrifice to Apollo on behalf of the Danaans, that we may propitiate the god, who has now brought sorrow upon the Argives."

So saying he gave the girl over to her father, who received her gladly, and they ranged the holy hecatomb all orderly round the altar of the god. They washed their hands and took up the barley-meal to sprinkle over the victims, while Chryses lifted up his hands and prayed aloud on their behalf. "Hear me," he cried, "O god of the silver bow, that protectest Chryse and holy Cilla, and rulest Tenedos with thy might. Even as thou didst hear me aforetime when I prayed, and didst press hardly upon the Achaeans, so hear me yet again, and stay this fearful pestilence from the Danaans."

Thus did he pray, and Apollo heard his prayer. When they had done praying and sprinkling the barley-meal, they drew back the heads of the victims and killed and flayed them. When they had finished their work and the feast was ready, they ate it, and every man had his full share, so that all were satisfied. As soon as they had had enough to eat and drink, pages filled the mixing-bowl with wine and water and handed it round, after giving every man his drink-offering.

Thus all day long the young men worshipped the god with song, hymning him and chanting the joyous paean, and the god took pleasure in their voices; but when the sun went down, and it came on dark, they laid themselves down to sleep by the stern cables of the ship, and when the child of morning, rosy-fingered Dawn, appeared they again set sail for the host of the Achaeans. Apollo sent them a fair wind, so they raised their mast and hoisted their white sails aloft. As the sail bellied with the wind the ship flew through the deep blue water, and the foam hissed against her bows as she sped onward. When they reached the wide-stretching host of the Achaeans, they drew the vessel ashore, high and dry upon the sands, set her strong props beneath her, and went their ways to their own tents and ships.

But Achilles abode at his ships and nursed his anger. He went not to the honorable assembly, and sallied not forth to fight, but gnawed at his own heart, pining for battle and the war-cry.

HOMER
THE ODYSSEY

trans. Samuel Butler

Upon returning home from his 10-year journey, Ulysses remains true to his cunning nature and assumes a different identity to keep himself hidden from Penelope, the beloved wife he has been separated from for so long. During this episode from Book XIX, he thinly maintains his façade, discussing his own exploits and providing Penelope assurance that he is nearby. With this fascinating choice, he ends up uncovering approaches that will inform the structure of all stories to come: the importance of exaggeration and elision, the difficulty of returning home, the subtlety involved in constructing an identity, and, most importantly, that fiction is a means of approaching delicate, greater truths.

"I, who am the younger, am called Aethon; my brother, however, was at once the older and the more valiant of the two; hence it was in Crete that I saw Ulysses and showed him hospitality, for the winds took him there as he was on his way to Troy, carrying him out of his course from cape Malea and leaving him in Amnisus off the cave of Ilithuia, where the harbors are difficult to enter and he could hardly find shelter from the winds that were then raging. As soon as he got there he went into the town and asked for Idomeneus, claiming to be his old and valued friend, but Idomeneus had already set sail for Troy some ten or twelve days earlier, so I took him to my own house and showed him every kind of hospitality, for I had abundance of everything. Moreover, I fed the men who were with him with barley meal from the public store, and got subscriptions of wine and oxen for them to sacrifice to their heart's content. They stayed with me twelve days, for there was a gale blowing from the North so strong that one could hardly keep one's feet on land. I suppose some unfriendly god had raised it for them, but on the thirteenth day the wind dropped, and they got away."

Many a plausible tale did Ulysses further tell her, and Penelope wept as she listened, for her heart was melted. As the snow wastes upon the mountain tops when the winds from South East and West have breathed upon it and thawed it till the rivers run bank full with water, even so did her cheeks overflow with tears for the husband who was all the time sitting by her side. Ulysses felt for her and was sorry for her, but he kept his eyes as hard as horn or iron without letting them so much as quiver, so cunningly did he restrain his tears. Then, when she had relieved herself by weeping, she turned to him again and said: "Now, stranger, I shall put you to the test and see whether or no you really did entertain my husband and his men, as you say you did. Tell me, then, how he was dressed, what kind of a man he was to look at, and so also with his companions."

"Madam," answered Ulysses, "it is such a long time ago that I can hardly say. Twenty years are come and gone since he left my home, and went elsewhither; but I will tell you as well as I can recollect. Ulysses wore a mantle of purple wool, double lined, and it was fastened by a gold brooch with two catches for the pin. On the face of this there was a device that shewed a dog holding a spotted fawn between his fore paws, and watching it as it lay panting upon the ground. Every one marvelled at the way in which these things had been done in gold, the dog looking at the fawn, and strangling it, while the fawn was struggling convulsively to escape. As for the shirt that he wore next his skin, it was so soft that it fitted him like the skin of an onion, and glistened in the sunlight to the admiration of all the women who beheld it. Furthermore I say, and lay my saying to your heart, that I do not know whether Ulysses wore these clothes when he left home, or whether one of his companions had given them to him while he was on his voyage; or possibly some one at whose house he was staying made him a present of them, for he was a man of many friends and had few equals among the Achaeans. I myself gave him a sword of bronze and a beautiful purple mantle, double lined, with a shirt that went down to his feet, and I sent him on board his ship with every mark of honor. He had a servant with him, a little older than himself, and I can tell you what he was like; his shoulders were hunched, he was dark, and he had thick curly hair. His name was Eurybates, and Ulysses treated him with greater familiarity than he did any of the others, as being the most like-minded with himself."

Penelope was moved still more deeply as she heard the indisputable proofs that Ulysses laid before her; and when she had again found relief in tears she said to him, "Stranger, I was already disposed to pity you, but henceforth you shall be honored and made welcome in my house. It was I who gave Ulysses the clothes you speak of. I took them out of the store room and folded them up myself, and I gave him also the gold brooch to wear as an ornament. Alas! I shall never welcome him home again. It was by an ill fate that he ever set out for that detested city whose very name I cannot bring myself even to mention."

Then Ulysses answered, "Madam, wife of Ulysses, do not disfigure yourself further by grieving thus bitterly for your loss, though I can hardly blame you for doing so. A woman who has loved her husband and borne him children, would naturally be grieved at losing him, even though he were a worse man than Ulysses, who they say was like a god. Still, cease your tears and listen to what I can tell you. I will hide nothing from you, and can say with perfect truth that I have lately heard of Ulysses as being alive and on his way home; he is among the Thesprotians, and is bringing back much valuable treasure that he has begged from one and another of them; but his ship and all his crew were lost as they were leaving the Thrinacian island, for Jove and the sun-god were angry with him because his men had slaughtered the sun-god's cattle, and they were all drowned to a man. But Ulysses stuck to the keel of the ship and was drifted on to the land of the Phaeacians, who are near of kin to the immortals, and who treated him as though he had been a god, giving him many presents, and wishing to escort him home safe and sound. In fact Ulysses would have been here long ago, had he not thought better to go from land to land gathering wealth; for there is no man living who is so wily as he is; there is no one can compare with him.

"Pheidon king of the Thesprotians told me all this, and he swore to me—making drink-offerings in his house as he did so—that the ship was by the water side and the crew found who would take Ulysses to his own country. He sent me off first, for there happened to be a Thesprotian ship sailing for the wheat-growing island of Dulichium, but he showed me all the treasure Ulysses had got together, and he had enough lying in the house of king Pheidon to keep his family for ten generations; but the king said Ulysses had gone to Dodona that he might learn Jove's mind from the high oak tree, and know whether after so long an absence he should return to Ithaca openly or in secret. So you may know he is safe and will be here shortly; he is close at hand and cannot remain away from home much longer; nevertheless I will confirm my words with an oath, and call Jove who is the first and mightiest of all gods to witness, as also that hearth of Ulysses to which I have now come, that all I have spoken shall surely come to pass. Ulysses will return in this self same year; with the end of this moon and the beginning of the next he will be here."

"May it be even so," answered Penelope; "if your words come true you shall have such gifts and such good will from me that all who see you shall congratulate you; but I know very well how it will be. Ulysses will not return, neither will you get your escort hence, for so surely as that Ulysses ever was, there are now no longer any such masters in the house as he was, to receive honorable strangers or to further them on their way home."

BOOK OF GENESIS

King James Version

It is difficult to single out one individual or one story from the Old Testament, but as far as human thought is concerned, Joseph, he of the Technicolor Dreamcoat, is the chosen one. Before Joseph, God was restricted to those individuals He had revealed Himself directly to. Joseph, in interpreting the Pharaoh's dream, situates God in symbols. Suddenly, given humanity's inclination toward metaphor, everyone has been granted access to the divine.

And it came to pass at the end of two full years, that Pharaoh dreamed: and, behold, he stood by the river. And, behold, there came up out of the river seven well favored cattle and fatfleshed; and they fed in a meadow. And, behold, seven other cattle came up after them out of the river, ill favored and leanfleshed; and stood by the other cattle upon the brink of the river. And the ill favored and leanfleshed cattle did eat up the seven well favored and fat cattle. So Pharaoh awoke.

And he slept and dreamed the second time: and, behold, seven ears of corn came up upon one stalk, rank and good. And, behold, seven thin ears and blasted with the east wind sprung up after them. And the seven thin ears devoured the seven rank and full ears. And Pharaoh awoke, and, behold, it was a dream.

And it came to pass in the morning that his spirit was troubled; and he sent and called for all the magicians of Egypt, and all the wise men thereof: and Pharaoh told them his dream; but there was none that could interpret them unto Pharaoh.

Then spake the chief butler unto Pharaoh, saying, "I do remember my faults this day: Pharaoh was wroth with his servants, and put me in ward in the captain of the guard's house, both me and the chief baker: And we dreamed a dream in one night, I and he; we dreamed each man according to the interpretation of his dream.

"And there was there with us a young man, an Hebrew, servant to the captain of the guard; and we told him, and he interpreted to us our dreams; to each man according to his dream he did interpret. And it came to pass, as he interpreted to us, so it was; me he restored unto mine office, and him he hanged."

Then Pharaoh sent and called Joseph, and they brought him hastily out of the dungeon:

and he shaved himself, and changed his raiment, and came in unto Pharaoh. And Pharaoh said unto Joseph, "I have dreamed a dream, and there is none that can interpret it: and I have heard say of thee, that thou canst understand a dream to interpret it."

And Joseph answered Pharaoh, saying, "It is not in me: God shall give Pharaoh an answer of peace." And Pharaoh said unto Joseph, "In my dream, behold, I stood upon the bank of the river. And, behold, there came up out of the river seven cattle, fatfleshed and well favored; and they fed in a meadow. And, behold, seven other cattle came up after them, poor and very ill favored and leanfleshed, such as I never saw in all the land of Egypt for badness. And the lean and the ill favored cattle did eat up the first seven fat cattle. And when they had eaten them up, it could not be known that they had eaten them; but they were still ill favored, as at the beginning. So I awoke.

"And I saw in my dream, and, behold, seven ears came up in one stalk, full and good. And, behold, seven ears, withered, thin, and blasted with the east wind, sprung up after them. And the thin ears devoured the seven good ears: and I told this unto the magicians; but there was none that could declare it to me."

And Joseph said unto Pharaoh, "The dream of Pharaoh is one: God hath shewed Pharaoh what he is about to do.

"The seven good cattle are seven years; and the seven good ears are seven years: the dream is one.

"And the seven thin and ill favored cattle that came up after them are seven years; and the seven empty ears blasted with the east wind shall be seven years of famine.

"This is the thing which I have spoken unto Pharaoh: What God is about to do he sheweth unto Pharaoh.

"Behold, there come seven years of great plenty throughout all the land of Egypt:

And there shall arise after them seven years of famine; and all the plenty shall be forgotten in the land of Egypt; and the famine shall consume the land; And the plenty shall not be known in the land by reason of that famine following; for it shall be very grievous.

"And for that the dream was doubled unto Pharaoh twice; it is because the thing is established by God, and God will shortly bring it to pass.

"Now therefore let Pharaoh look out a man discreet and wise, and set him over the land of Egypt. Let Pharaoh do this, and let him appoint officers over the land, and take up the fifth part of the land of Egypt in the seven plenteous years.

"And let them gather all the food of those good years that come, and lay up corn under the hand of Pharaoh, and let them keep food in the cities. And that food shall be for store to the land against the seven years of famine, which shall be in the land of Egypt; that the land perish not through the famine."

And the thing was good in the eyes of Pharaoh, and in the eyes of all his servants.

And Pharaoh said unto his servants, "Can we find such a one as this is, a man in whom the Spirit of God is?" And Pharaoh said unto Joseph, "Forasmuch as God hath shewed thee all this, there is none so discreet and wise as thou art: Thou shalt be over my house, and according unto thy word shall all my people be ruled: only in the throne will I be greater than thou."

And Pharaoh said unto Joseph, "See, I have set thee over all the land of Egypt."

BHAGAVAD GITA

trans. Sir Edwin Arnold

This dialogue between the Panadava prince Arjuna and his guide Krishna is part of the Hindu epic, The Mahabharata. *With Arjuna hesitant to fight in battle because of the damage his actions will cause, Krishna assures him that he cannot really do any harm: he will only be disposing of his opponents' physical bodies; their souls, which are immortal, will move on to other hosts. In classifying the material world as ultimately inconsequential, and outlining the transcendent nature of the divine, the spectrum of what can come of human enterprise—both good and bad— undergoes a tremendous expansion.*

CHAPTER XIII

The elements, the conscious life, the mind,
The unseen vital force, the nine strange gates
Of the body, and the five domains of sense;
Desire, dislike, pleasure and pain, and thought
    Deep-woven, and persistency of being;
These all are wrought on Matter by the Soul!

Humbleness, truthfulness, and harmlessness,
    Patience and honor, reverence for the wise.
    Purity, constancy, control of self,
    Contempt of sense-delights, self-sacrifice,
        Perception of the certitude of ill
In birth, death, age, disease, suffering, and sin;
    Detachment, lightly holding unto home,
Children, and wife, and all that bindeth men;
    An ever-tranquil heart in fortunes good
    And fortunes evil, with a will set firm
    To worship Me—Me only! ceasing not;
Loving all solitudes, and shunning noise

Of foolish crowds; endeavors resolute
To reach perception of the Utmost Soul,
And grace to understand what gain it were
So to attain,—this is true Wisdom, Prince!
And what is otherwise is ignorance!

Now will I speak of knowledge best to know—
That Truth which giveth man Amrit to drink,
The Truth of Him, the Para-Brahm, the All,
The Uncreated; not Asat, nor Sat,
Not Form, nor the Unformed; yet both, and more;—
Whose hands are everywhere, and everywhere
Planted His feet, and everywhere His eyes
Beholding, and His ears in every place
Hearing, and all His faces everywhere
Enlightening and encompassing His worlds.
Glorified in the senses He hath given,
Yet beyond sense He is; sustaining all,
Yet dwells He unattached: of forms and modes
Master, yet neither form nor mode hath He;
He is within all beings—and without—
Motionless, yet still moving; not discerned
For subtlety of instant presence; close
To all, to each; yet measurelessly far!

Not manifold, and yet subsisting still
In all which lives; for ever to be known
As the Sustainer, yet, at the End of Times,
He maketh all to end—and re-creates.
The Light of Lights He is, in the heart of the Dark
Shining eternally. Wisdom He is
And Wisdom's way, and Guide of all the wise,
Planted in every heart.

So have I told
Of Life's stuff, and the moulding, and the lore
To comprehend. Whoso, adoring Me,
Perceiveth this, shall surely come to Me!

Know thou that Nature and the Spirit both
Have no beginning! Know that qualities
And changes of them are by Nature wrought;
That Nature puts to work the acting frame,
But Spirit doth inform it, and so cause
Feeling of pain and pleasure. Spirit, linked
To molded matter, entereth into bond
With qualities by Nature framed, and, thus
Married to matter, breeds the birth again
In good or evil yonis.

Yet is this—
Yea! in its bodily prison!—Spirit pure,
Spirit supreme; surveying, governing,
Guarding, possessing; Lord and Master still
Purusha, Ultimate, One Soul with Me.

Whoso thus knows himself, and knows his soul
Purusha, working through the qualities
With Nature's modes, the light hath come for him!
Whatever flesh he bears, never again
Shall he take on its load. Some few there be
By meditation find the Soul in Self
Self-schooled; and some by long philosophy
And holy life reach thither; some by works:
Some, never so attaining, hear of light
From other lips, and seize, and cleave to it
Worshipping; yea! and those—to teaching true—
Overpass Death!
Wherever, Indian Prince!
Life is—of moving things, or things unmoved,
Plant or still seed—know, what is there hath grown
By bond of Matter and of Spirit: Know
He sees indeed who sees in all alike
The living, lordly Soul; the Soul Supreme,
Imperishable amid the Perishing:

For, whoso thus beholds, in every place,
In every form, the same, one, Living Life,
Doth no more wrongfulness unto himself,
But goes the highest road which brings to bliss.
Seeing, he sees, indeed, who sees that works
Are Nature's wont, for Soul to practise by
Acting, yet not the agent; sees the mass
Of separate living things—each of its kind—
Issue from One, and blend again to One:
Then hath he Brahma, he attains!
O Prince!
That Ultimate, High Spirit, Uncreate,
Unqualified, even when it entereth flesh
Taketh no stain of acts, worketh in nought!
Like to th' ethereal air, pervading all,
Which, for sheer subtlety, avoideth taint,
The subtle Soul sits everywhere, unstained:
Like to the light of the all-piercing sun
Which is not changed by aught it shines upon,
The Soul's light shineth pure in every place;
And they who, by such eye of wisdom, see
How Matter, and what deals with it, divide;
And how the Spirit and the flesh have strife,
Those wise ones go the way which leads to Life!

PLATO
THE REPUBLIC

trans. Benjamin Jowett

On its face, Plato's famous allegory of the cave and its argument for the supremacy of a life spent considering the eternal seems little more than an attempt to validate himself, and his life's pursuit. But in a universe underpinned by invisible forces and particles, at a time where phenomena are mediated and skewed through representation, reproductions, and technology, we find that his vision was crystal clear during this reflection on the true nature of things, and the lowly state humanity defaults to.

❧

❧

Socrates: And now, let me show in a figure how far our nature is enlightened or un-enlightened—Behold! human beings living in a underground den, which has a mouth open toward the light and reaching all along the den; here they have been from their childhood, and have their legs and necks chained so that they cannot move, and can only see before them, being prevented by the chains from turning round their heads. Above and behind them a fire is blazing at a distance, and between the fire and the prisoners there is a raised way; and you will see, if you look, a low wall built along the way, like the screen which marionette players have in front of them, over which they show the puppets.

Glaucon: I see.

S: And do you see men passing along the wall carrying all sorts of vessels, and statues and figures of animals made of wood and stone and various materials, which appear over the wall? Some of them are talking, others silent.

G: You have shown me a strange image, and they are strange prisoners.

S: Like ourselves; and they see only their own shadows, or the shadows of one another, which the fire throws on the opposite wall of the cave?

G: True; how could they see anything but the shadows if they were never allowed to move their heads?

S: And of the objects which are being carried in like manner they would only see the shadows?

G: Yes.

S: And if they were able to converse with one another, would they not suppose that they were naming what was actually before them?

G: Very true.

S: And suppose further that the prison had an echo which came from the other side, would they not be sure to fancy when one of the passersby spoke that the voice which they heard came from the passing shadow?

G: No question.

S: To them the truth would be literally nothing but the shadows of the images.

G: That is certain.

S: And now look again, and see what will naturally follow if the prisoners are released and disabused of their error. At first, when any of them is liberated and compelled suddenly to stand up and turn his neck round and walk and look towards the light, he will suffer sharp pains; the glare will distress him, and he will be unable to see the realities of which in his former state he had seen the shadows; and then conceive some one saying to him, that what he saw before was an illusion, but that now, when he is approaching nearer to being and his eye is turned towards more real existence, he has a clearer vision—what will be his reply? And you may further imagine that his instructor is pointing to the objects as they pass and requiring him to name them—will he not be perplexed? Will he not fancy that the shadows which he formerly saw are truer than the objects which are now shown to him?

G: Far truer.

S: And if he is compelled to look straight at the light, will he not have a pain in his eyes which will make him turn away to take refuge in the objects of vision which he can see, and which he will conceive to be in reality clearer than the things which are now being shown to him?

G: True.

S: And suppose once more, that he is reluctantly dragged up a steep and rugged ascent, and held fast until he is forced into the presence of the sun himself, is he not likely to be pained and irritated? When he approaches the light his eyes will be dazzled, and he will not be able to see anything at all of what are now called realities.

G: Not all in a moment.

S: He will require to grow accustomed to the sight of the upper world. And first he will see the shadows best, next the reflections of men and other objects in the water, and then the objects themselves; then he will gaze upon the light of the moon and the stars and the spangled heaven; and he will see the sky and the stars by night better than the sun or the light of the sun by day?

G: Certainly.

S: Last of all he will be able to see the sun, and not mere reflections of him in the water, but he will see him in his own proper place, and not in another; and he will contemplate him as he is.

G: Certainly.

S: He will then proceed to argue that this is he who gives the season and the years, and is the guardian of all that is in the visible world, and in a certain way the cause of all things which he and his fellows have been accustomed to behold?

G: Clearly, he would first see the sun and then reason about him.

S: And when he remembered his old habitation, and the wisdom of the den and his fellow prisoners, do you not suppose that he would felicitate himself on the change, and pity them?

G: Certainly, he would.

S: And if they were in the habit of conferring honors among themselves on those who were quickest to observe the passing shadows and to remark which of them went before, and which followed after, and which were together; and who were therefore best able to draw conclusions as to the future, do you think that he would care for such honors and glories, or envy the possessors of them? Would he not say with Homer, "Better to be the poor servant of a poor master," and to endure anything, rather than think as they do and live after their manner?

G: Yes, I think that he would rather suffer anything than entertain these false notions and live in this miserable manner.

S: Imagine once more such an one coming suddenly out of the sun to be replaced in his old situation; would he not be certain to have his eyes full of darkness?

G: To be sure.

S: And if there were a contest, and he had to compete in measuring the shadows with the prisoners who had never moved out of the den, while his sight was still weak, and before his eyes had become steady (and the time which would be needed to acquire this new habit of sight might be very considerable), would he not be ridiculous? Men would say of him that up he went and down he came without his eyes; and that it was better not even to think of ascending; and if any one tried to loose another and lead him up to the light, let them only catch the offender, and they would put him to death.

G: No question.

S: This entire allegory you may now append, dear Glaucon, to the previous argument; the prison-house is the world of sight, the light of the fire is the sun, and you will not misapprehend me if you interpret the journey upwards to be the ascent of the soul into the intellectual world according to my poor belief, which, at your desire, I have expressed— whether rightly or wrongly God knows. But, whether true or false, my opinion is that in the world of knowledge the idea of good appears last of all, and is seen only with an effort; and, when seen, is also inferred to be the universal author of all things beautiful and right, parent of light and of the lord of light in this visible world, and the immediate source of reason and truth in the intellectual; and that this is the power upon which he who would act rationally either in public or private life must have his eye fixed.

G: I agree as far as I am able to understand you.

S: Moreover, you must not wonder that those who attain to this beatific vision are unwilling to descend to human affairs; for their souls are ever hastening into the upper world where they desire to dwell; which desire of theirs is very natural, if our allegory may be trusted.

DISCOVERING

OURSELVES

SAINT AUGUSTINE
CONFESSIONS

trans. E. B. Pusey

Considering that it did much to establish original sin as a fundamental piece of human existence and posited the mercy of God as the only way out, one would not expect to find man's wondrous capabilities lionized in Saint Augustine's Confessions. *But Augustine does just that during Book XI's examination of time. In speculating that it is only in the human mind that time can be measured, he outlines consciousness as something boundless, and positions it as a universe in itself.*

Courage, my mind, and press on mightily. God is our helper, He made us, and not we ourselves. Press on where truth begins to dawn. Suppose, now, the voice of a body begins to sound, and does sound, and sounds on, and list, it ceases; it is silence now, and that voice is past, and is no more a voice. Before it sounded, it was to come, and could not be measured, because as yet it was not, and now it cannot, because it is no longer. Then therefore while it sounded, it might; because there then was what might be measured. But yet even then it was not at a stay; for it was passing on, and passing away. Could it be measured the rather, for that? For while passing, it was being extended into some space of time, so that it might be measured, since the present hath no space. If therefore then it might, then, lo, suppose another voice hath begun to sound, and still soundeth in one continued tenor without any interruption; let us measure it while it sounds; seeing when it hath left sounding, it will then be past, and nothing left to be measured; let us measure it verily, and tell how much it is. But it sounds still, nor can it be measured but from the instant it began in, unto the end it left in. For the very space between is the thing we measure, namely, from some beginning unto some end. Wherefore, a voice that is not yet ended, cannot be measured, so that it may be said how long, or short it is; nor can it be called equal to another, or double to a single, or the like. But when ended, it no longer is. How may it then be measured? And yet we measure times; but yet neither those which are not yet, nor those which no longer are, nor those which are not lengthened out by some pause, nor those which have no bounds. We measure neither times to come, nor past, nor present, nor passing; and yet we do measure times.

"Deus Creator omnium," this verse of eight syllables alternates between short and long syllables. The four short then, the first, third, fifth, and seventh, are but single, in respect of the four long, the second, fourth, sixth, and eighth. Every one of these to every one of those, hath a double time: I pronounce them, report on them, and find it so, as one's plain sense perceives. By plain sense then, I measure a long syllable by a short, and I sensibly find it to have twice so much; but when one sounds after the other, if the former be short, the latter long, how shall I detain the short one, and how, measuring, shall I apply it to the long, that I may find this to have twice so much; seeing the long does not begin to sound, unless the short leaves sounding? And that very long one do I measure as present, seeing I measure it not till it be ended? Now his ending is his passing away. What then is it I measure? where is the short syllable by which I measure? where the long which I measure? Both have sounded, have flown, passed away, are no more; and yet I measure, and confidently answer (so far as is presumed on a practised sense) that as to space of time this syllable is but single, that double. And yet I could not do this, unless they were already past and ended.

It is not then themselves, which now are not, that I measure, but something in my memory, which there remains fixed.

It is in thee, my mind, that I measure times. Interrupt me not, that is, interrupt not thyself with the tumults of thy impressions. In thee I measure times; the impression, which things as they pass by cause in thee, remains even when they are gone; this it is which still present, I measure, not the things which pass by to make this impression. This I measure, when I measure times. Either then this is time, or I do not measure times. What when we measure silence, and say that this silence hath held as long time as did that voice? do we not stretch out our thought to the measure of a voice, as if it sounded, that so we may be able to report of the intervals of silence in a given space of time? For though both voice and tongue be still, yet in thought we go over poems, and verses, and any other discourse, or dimensions of motions, and report as to the spaces of times, how much this is in respect of that, no otherwise than if vocally we did pronounce them. If a man would utter a lengthened sound, and had settled in thought how long it should be, he hath in silence already gone through a space of time, and committing it to memory, begins to utter that speech, which sounds on, until it be brought unto the end proposed. Yea it hath sounded, and will sound; for so much of it as is finished, hath sounded already, and the rest will sound. And thus passeth it on, until the present intent conveys over the future into the past; the past increasing by the diminution of the future, until by the consumption of the future, all is past.

But how is that future diminished or consumed, which as yet is not? or how that past increased, which is now no longer, save that in the mind which enacteth this, there be three things done? For it expects, it considers, it remembers; that so that which it expecteth, through that which it considereth, passeth into that which it remembereth. Who therefore denieth, that things to come are not as yet?

and yet, there is in the mind an expectation of things to come. And who denies past things to be now no longer? and yet is there still in the mind a memory of things past. And who denieth the present time hath no space, because it passeth away in a moment? and yet our consideration continueth, through which that which shall be present proceedeth to become absent. It is not then future time, that is long, for as yet it is not: but a long future, is "a long expectation of the future," nor is it time past, which now is not, that is long; but a long past, is "a long memory of the past."

I am about to repeat a Psalm that I know. Before I begin, my expectation is extended over the whole; but when I have begun, how much soever of it I shall separate off into the past, is extended along my memory; thus the life of this action of mine is divided between my memory as to what I have repeated, and expectation as to what I am about to repeat; but "consideration" is present with me, that through it what was future, may be conveyed over, so as to become past. Which the more it is done again and again, so much the more the expectation being shortened, is the memory enlarged: till the whole expectation be at length exhausted, when that whole action being ended, shall have passed into memory. And this which takes place in the whole Psalm, the same takes place in each several portion of it, and each several syllable; the same holds in that longer action, whereof this Psalm may be part; the same holds in the whole life of man, whereof all the actions of man are parts; the same holds through the whole age of the sons of men, whereof all the lives of men are parts.

SUN TZU
THE ART OF WAR

trans. Lionel Giles

By drilling deep into the practical, Sun Tzu managed to access the universal. While this famous book of military strategy remains a vital text in that arena, it has resonated far beyond the battlefield. Everyone from revolutionaries like Mao Zedong to Fortune 500 CEOs and sports personages such as Bill Belichick have cited its penetrating insights as foundational to their approach and successes. The wide applications of its meditations upon the importance of self-knowledge, cunning, and flexibility, and the power of the collective over the individual, are testaments to the quality of Sun Tzu's mind, but also to the combative element that inheres in much of human interaction.

BOOK IV: TACTICAL DISPOSITIONS

The good fighters of old first put themselves beyond the possibility of defeat, and then waited for an opportunity of defeating the enemy.

To secure ourselves against defeat lies in our own hands, but the opportunity of defeating the enemy is provided by the enemy himself.

Standing on the defensive indicates insufficient strength; attacking, a superabundance of strength.

The skillful fighter puts himself into a position which makes defeat impossible, and does not miss the moment for defeating the enemy.

Thus it is that in war the victorious strategist only seeks battle after the victory has been won, whereas he who is destined to defeat first fights and afterwards looks for victory.

BOOK V: ENERGY

The control of a large force is the same principle as the control of a few men: it is merely a question of dividing up their numbers.

In all fighting, the direct method may be used for joining battle, but indirect methods will be needed in order to secure victory.

Indirect tactics, efficiently applied, are inexhaustible as Heaven and Earth, unending as the flow of rivers and streams; like the sun and moon, they end but to begin anew; like the four seasons, they pass away to return once more.

There are not more than five musical notes, yet the combinations of these five give rise to more melodies than can ever be heard.

In battle, there are not more than two methods of attack—the direct and the indirect; yet these two in combination give rise to an endless series of maneuvers.

Simulated disorder postulates perfect discipline, simulated fear postulates courage; simulated weakness postulates strength.

Thus one who is skillful at keeping the enemy on the move maintains deceitful appearances, according to which the enemy will act. He sacrifices something, that the enemy may snatch at it.

The clever combatant looks to the effect of combined energy, and does not require too much from individuals. Hence his ability to pick out the right men and utilize combined energy.

BOOK VI: WEAK POINTS AND STRONG

You can be sure of succeeding in your attacks if you only attack places which are undefended. You can ensure the safety of your defense if you only hold positions that cannot be attacked.

Numerical weakness comes from having to prepare against possible attacks; numerical strength, from compelling our adversary to make these preparations against us.

How victory may be produced for them out of the enemy's own tactics—that is what the multitude cannot comprehend.

All men can see the tactics whereby I conquer, but what none can see is the strategy out of which victory is evolved.

Water shapes its course according to the nature of the ground over which it flows; the soldier works out his victory in relation to the foe whom he is facing.

Therefore, just as water retains no constant shape, so in warfare there are no constant conditions.

He who can modify his tactics in relation to his opponent and thereby succeed in winning, may be called a heaven-born captain.

BOOK VII: MANEUVERING

When you plunder a countryside, let the spoil be divided amongst your men; when you capture new territory, cut it up into allotments for the benefit of the soldiery.

He will conquer who has learnt the artifice of deviation. Such is the art of maneuvering.

Now a soldier's spirit is keenest in the morning; by noonday it has begun to flag; and in the evening, his mind is bent only on returning to camp.

A clever general, therefore, avoids an army when its spirit is keen, but attacks it when it is sluggish and inclined to return. This is the art of studying moods.

Disciplined and calm, to await the appearance of disorder and hubbub amongst the enemy—this is the art of retaining self-possession.

To refrain from intercepting an enemy whose banners are in perfect order, to refrain from attacking an army drawn up in calm and confident array: this is the art of studying circumstances.

When you surround an army, leave an outlet free. Do not press a desperate foe too hard.

BOOK VIII: VARIATION IN TACTICS

There are roads which must not be followed, armies which must be not attacked, towns which must not be besieged, positions which must not be contested, commands of the sovereign which must not be obeyed.

The general who thoroughly understands the advantages that accompany variation of tactics knows how to handle his troops.

Hence in the wise leader's plans, considerations of advantage and of disadvantage will be blended together.

The art of war teaches us to rely not on the likelihood of the enemy's not coming, but on our own readiness to receive him; not on the chance of his not attacking, but rather on the fact that we have made our position unassailable.

There are five dangerous faults which may affect a general: recklessness, which leads to destruction; cowardice, which leads to capture; a hasty temper, which can be provoked by insults; a delicacy of honor which is sensitive to shame; over-solicitude for his men, which exposes him to worry and trouble.

MARCO POLO AND RUSTICHELLO OF PISA
THE TRAVELS OF MARCO POLO

trans. Henry Yule

The first sign of light after a long period of darkness. Polo's tale of his journey to the Far East became a global sensation on the strength of fantastical details such as a pasta-bearing plant and islanders with the heads of dogs. But it is also a watershed moment in the development of capitalism. In continually alerting merchants to the agreeable conditions and considerable opportunities in China, and extolling Emperor Kublai Khan's revolutionary banking practices, Polo got the West to believe that the world was well worth exploring.

CHAPTER XXII

You must know that the city of Cambaluc hath such a multitude of houses, and such a vast population inside the walls and outside, that it seems quite past all possibility. There is a suburb outside each of the gates, which are twelve in number; and these suburbs are so great that they contain more people than the city itself, for the suburb of one gate spreads in width till it meets the suburb of the next, whilst they extend in length some three or four miles. In those suburbs lodge the foreign merchants and travelers, of whom there are always great numbers who have come to bring presents to the Emperor, or to sell articles at Court, or because the city affords so good a mart to attract traders. There are in each of the suburbs, to a distance of a mile from the city, numerous fine hostelries for the lodgment of merchants from different parts of the world, and a special hostelry is assigned to each description of people, as if we should say there is one for the Lombards, another for the Germans, and a third for the Frenchmen. And thus there are as many good houses outside of the city as inside, without counting those that belong to the great lords and barons, which are very numerous.

You must know that it is forbidden to bury any dead body inside the city. If the body be that of an Idolater it is carried out beyond the city and suburbs to a remote place assigned for the purpose, to be burnt. And if it be of one belonging to a religion the custom of which is to bury, such as the Christian, the Saracen, or what not, it is also carried out beyond the suburbs to a distant place assigned for the purpose. And thus the city is preserved in a better and more healthy state.

Moreover, no public woman resides inside the city, but all such abide outside in the suburbs. And 'tis wonderful what a vast number of these there are for the foreigners; it is a certain fact that there are more than 20,000 of them living by prostitution. And that so many can live in this way will show you how vast is the population.

Guards patrol the city every night in parties of 30 or 40, looking out for any persons who may be abroad at unseasonable hours, i.e. after the great bell hath stricken thrice. If they find any such person he is immediately taken to prison, and examined next morning by the proper officers. If these find him guilty of any misdemeanor they order him a proportionate beating with the stick. Under this punishment people sometimes die; but they adopt it in order to eschew bloodshed; for their *Bacsis* (a conjurer or medicine man in Polo's tale) say that it is an evil thing to shed man's blood.

To this city also are brought articles of greater cost and rarity, and in greater abundance of all kinds, than to any other city in the world. For people of every description, and from every region, bring things (including all the costly wares of India, as well as the fine and precious goods of Cathay itself with its provinces), some for the sovereign, some for the court, some for the city which is so great, some for the crowds of Barons and Knights, some for the great hosts of the Emperor which are quartered round about; and thus between court and city the quantity brought in is endless.

As a sample, I tell you, no day in the year passes that there do not enter the city 1000 cart-loads of silk alone, from which are made quantities of cloth of silk and gold, and of other goods. And this is not to be wondered at; for in all the countries round about there is no flax, so that everything has to be made of silk. It is true, indeed, that in some parts of the country there is cotton and hemp, but not sufficient for their wants. This, however, is not of much consequence, because silk is so abundant and cheap, and is a more valuable substance than either flax or cotton.

Round about this great city of Cambaluc there are some 200 other cities at various distances, from which traders come to sell their goods and buy others for their lords; and all find means to make their sales and purchases, so that the traffic of the city is passing great.

CHAPTER XXIV

Now that I have told you in detail of the splendor of this City of the Emperor's, I shall proceed to tell you of the Mint which he hath in the same city, in the which he hath his money coined and struck, as I shall relate to you. And in doing so I shall make manifest to you how it is that the Great Lord may well be able to accomplish even much more than I have told you, or am going to tell you, in this Book. For, tell it how I might, you never would be satisfied that I was keeping within truth and reason!

The Emperor's Mint then is in this same City of Cambaluc, and the way it is wrought is such that you might say he hath the Secret of Alchemy in perfection, and you would be right! For he makes his money after this fashion.

He makes them take of the bark of a certain tree, in fact of the Mulberry Tree, the leaves of which are the food of the silkworms—these trees being so numerous that whole districts are full of them. What they take is a certain fine white bast or skin which lies between the wood of the tree and the thick outer bark, and this they make into something resembling sheets of paper, but black. When these sheets have been prepared they are cut up into pieces of different sizes. The smallest of these sizes is worth a half tornesel; the next, a little larger, one tornesel; one, a little larger still, is worth half a silver groat of Venice; another a whole groat; others yet two groats, five groats, and ten groats. There is also a kind worth one Bezant of gold, and others of three Bezants, and so up to ten. All these pieces of paper are issued with as much solemnity and authority as if they were of pure gold or silver; and on every piece a variety of officials, whose duty it is, have to write their names, and to put their seals. And when all is prepared duly, the chief officer deputed by the Kaan smears the Seal entrusted to him with vermilion, and impresses it on the paper, so that the form of the Seal remains printed upon it in red; the Money is then authentic. Any one forging it would be punished with death. And the Kaan causes every year to be made such a vast quantity of this money, which costs him nothing, that it must equal in amount all the treasure in the world.

With these pieces of paper, made as I have described, he causes all payments on his own account to be made; and he makes them to pass current universally over all his kingdoms and provinces and territories, and whithersoever his power and sovereignty extends. And nobody, however important he may think himself, dares to refuse them on pain of death. And indeed everybody takes them readily, for wheresoever a person may go throughout the Great Kaan's dominions he shall find these pieces of paper current, and shall be able to transact all sales and purchases of goods by means of them just as well as if they were coins of pure gold. And all the while they are so light that ten bezants' worth does not weigh one golden bezant.

Furthermore all merchants arriving from India or other countries, and bringing with them gold or silver or gems and pearls, are prohibited from selling to any one but the Emperor. He has twelve experts chosen for this business, men of shrewdness and experience in such affairs; these appraise the articles, and the Emperor then pays a liberal price for them in those pieces of paper. The merchants accept his price readily, for in the first place they would not get so good an one from anybody else, and secondly they are paid without any delay. And with this paper-money they can buy what they like anywhere over the Empire, whilst it is also vastly lighter to carry about on their journeys. And it is a truth that the merchants will several times in the year bring wares to the amount of 400,000 bezants, and the Grand Sire pays for all in that paper. So he buys such a quantity of those precious things every year that his treasure is endless, while all the time the money he pays away costs him nothing at all. Moreover, several times in the year proclamation is made through the city that any one who may have gold or silver or gems or pearls, by taking them to the Mint shall get a handsome price for them. And the owners are glad to do this, because they would find no other purchaser give so large a price. Thus the quantity they bring in is marvellous, though these who do not choose to do so may let it alone. Still, in this way, nearly all the valuables in the country come into the Kaan's possession.

When any of those pieces of paper are spoiled—not that they are so very flimsy neither—the owner carries them to the Mint, and by paying three per cent, on the value he gets new pieces in exchange. And if any Baron, or any one else soever, hath need of gold or silver or gems or pearls, in order to make plate, or girdles, or the like, he goes to the Mint and buys as much as he list, paying in this paper-money.

Now you have heard the ways and means whereby the Great Kaan may have, and in fact *has*, more treasure than all the Kings in the World; and you know all about it and the reason why. And now I will tell you of the great Dignitaries which act in this city on behalf of the Emperor.

GEOFFREY CHAUCER
THE CANTERBURY TALES

It only looks like it's from another world. Once you accustom yourself to the Middle English, you'll see that Chaucer's magnum opus is alternately as bawdy and intent on exposing hypocrisy as the standard social media feed. In this famous snippet from the Wife of Bath's Prologue, Chaucer sheds light on the double standard that allows multiple marriages to leave no mark on the character of a great man while instantly bringing disgrace to a woman. This, in addition to its argument for the value of personal experience over authoritative abstractions and plea for the acceptance of the natural, keeps The Canterbury Tales remarkably refreshing.

THE WIFE OF BATH'S PROLOGUE

Experience, though noon auctoritee
Were in this world, were right y-nough to me
To speke of wo that is in mariage;
For, lordinges, sith I twelf yeer was of age,
Thonked be god that is eterne on lyve,
Housbondes at chirche-dore I have had fyve;
For I so ofte have y-wedded be;
And alle were worthy men in hir degree.
But me was told certeyn, nat longe agon is,
That sith that Crist ne wente never but onis
To wedding in the Cane of Galilee,
That by the same ensample taughte he me
That I ne sholde wedded be but ones.
Herke eek, lo! which a sharp word for the nones
Besyde a welle Iesus, god and man,
Spak in repreve of the Samaritan:
"Thou hast y-had fyve housbondes," quod he,
"And thilke man, the which that hath now thee,
Is noght thyn housbond;" thus seyde he certeyn;
What that he mente ther-by, I can nat seyn;

But that I axe, why that the fifthe man
Was noon housbond to the Samaritan?
How manye mighte she have in mariage?
Yet herde I never tellen in myn age
Upon this nombre diffinicioun;
Men may devyne and glosen up and doun.
But wel I woot expres, with-oute lye,
God bad us for to wexe and multiplye;
That gentil text can I wel understonde.
Eek wel I woot he seyde, myn housbonde
Sholde lete fader and moder, and take me;
But of no nombre mencioun made he,
Of bigamye or of octogamye;
Why sholde men speke of it vileinye?

Lo, here the wyse king, dan Salomon;
I trowe he hadde wyves mo than oon;
As, wolde god, it leveful were to me
To be refresshed half so ofte as he!
Which yifte of god hadde he for alle his wyvis!
No man hath swich, that in this world alyve is.
God woot, this noble king, as to my wit,
The firste night had many a mery fit
With ech of hem, so wel was him on lyve!

Blessed be god that I have wedded fyve!
Welcome the sixte, whan that ever he shal.
For sothe, I wol nat kepe me chast in al;
Whan myn housbond is fro the world y-gon,
Som Cristen man shal wedde me anon;
For thanne thapostle seith, that I am free
To wedde, a goddes half, wher it lyketh me.
He seith that to be wedded is no sinne;
Bet is to be wedded than to brinne.
What rekketh me, thogh folk seye vileinye
Of shrewed Lameth and his bigamye?
I woot wel Abraham was an holy man,
And Iacob eek, as forforth as I can;
And ech of hem hadde wyves mo than two;
And many another holy man also.
Whan saugh ye ever, in any maner age,
That hye god defended mariage
By expres word? I pray you, telleth me;
Or wher comanded he virginitee?
I woot as wel as ye, it is no drede,
Thapostel, whan he speketh of maydenhede;
He seyde, that precept ther-of hadde he noon.
Men may conseille a womman to been oon,
But conseilling is no comandement;

He putte it in our owene Iugement.
For hadde god comanded maydenhede,
Thanne hadde he dampned wedding with the dede;
And certes, if ther were no seed y-sowe,
Virginitee, wher-of than sholde it growe?
Poul dorste nat comanden atte leste
A thing of which his maister yaf noon heste.
The dart is set up for virginitee;
Cacche who so may, who renneth best lat see.

WILLIAM SHAKESPEARE
HAMLET

Notice how different this feels from the theatrics and dissembling Ulysses involved himself in during the excerpt from The Odyssey *(see page 20). In* Hamlet *we can see humanity becoming both more remote and more self-involved, a paradoxical bind that leaves one paralyzed by their interior state and then spurred to elaborate, puzzling action. Disgusted by the prospect of talking about his feelings, and incapable of acting upon them, Hamlet finds an outlet in artifice—but the play he will put on feels as much about realizing a dark and amorphous urge as it is intended to discover the truth. Within this and his other asides, one can sense the nascence of the "I," the idiosyncratic subjectivity that fuels so much of culture today.*

O what a rogue and peasant slave am I!
Is it not monstrous that this player here,
But in a fiction, in a dream of passion,
Could force his soul so to his own conceit
That from her working all his visage wan'd;
Tears in his eyes, distraction in's aspect,
A broken voice, and his whole function suiting
With forms to his conceit? And all for nothing!
For Hecuba?
What's Hecuba to him, or he to Hecuba,
That he should weep for her? What would he do,
Had he the motive and the cue for passion
That I have? He would drown the stage with tears
And cleave the general ear with horrid speech;
Make mad the guilty, and appal the free,
Confound the ignorant, and amaze indeed,
The very faculties of eyes and ears. Yet I,
A dull and muddy-mettled rascal, peak
Like John-a-dreams, unpregnant of my cause,
And can say nothing. No, not for a king
Upon whose property and most dear life
A damn'd defeat was made. Am I a coward?

Who calls me villain, breaks my pate across?
Plucks off my beard and blows it in my face?
Tweaks me by the nose, gives me the lie i' th' throat
As deep as to the lungs? Who does me this?
Ha! 'Swounds, I should take it: for it cannot be
But I am pigeon-liver'd, and lack gall
To make oppression bitter, or ere this
I should have fatted all the region kites
With this slave's offal. Bloody, bawdy villain!
Remorseless, treacherous, lecherous, kindless villain!
Oh vengeance!
Why, what an ass am I! This is most brave,
That I, the son of a dear father murder'd,
Prompted to my revenge by heaven and hell,
Must, like a whore, unpack my heart with words
And fall a-cursing like a very drab,
A scullion! Fie upon't! Foh!
About, my brain! I have heard
That guilty creatures sitting at a play,
Have by the very cunning of the scene,
Been struck so to the soul that presently
They have proclaim'd their malefactions.
For murder, though it have no tongue, will speak
With most miraculous organ. I'll have these players

Play something like the murder of my father
Before mine uncle. I'll observe his looks;
I'll tent him to the quick. If he but blench,
I know my course. The spirit that I have seen
May be the devil, and the devil hath power
T'assume a pleasing shape, yea, and perhaps
Out of my weakness and my melancholy,
As he is very potent with such spirits,
Abuses me to damn me. I'll have grounds
More relative than this. The play's the thing
Wherein I'll catch the conscience of the King.

THOMAS HOBBES
LEVIATHAN

Desperate to find some way to avoid returning to the chaos caused by the English Civil War, Hobbes methodically maps out the grim road that led to it: a State of Nature, where each individual has the right "to all things," and can pursue whatever one judges necessary for their own preservation. As Hobbes sees it, the only way out of this hopelessness is for each individual to give themselves over entirely to the sovereign of the state, who will provide security and stability in exchange for being made as infallible and omnipotent as a god. This early iteration of Big Brother frames the struggles that continue to dominate the discourse: individual against state, and public against private.

CHAPTER XVIII: OF THE RIGHTS OF SOVERAIGNES BY INSTITUTION

The Act Of Instituting A Common-wealth, What

A Common-wealth is said to be Instituted, when a Multitude of men do Agree, and Covenant, Every One With Every One, that to whatsoever Man, or Assembly Of Men, shall be given by the major part, the Right to Present the Person of them all, (that is to say, to be their Representative;) every one, as well he that Voted For It, as he that Voted Against It, shall Authorise all the Actions and Judgements, of that Man, or Assembly of men, in the same manner, as if they were his own, to the end, to live peaceably amongst themselves, and be protected against other men.

The Consequences To Such Institution, Are:

I. The Subjects Cannot Change
The Forme Of Government

From this Institution of a Common-wealth are derived all the Rights, and Facultyes of him, or them, on whom the Soveraigne Power is conferred by the consent of the People assembled.

First, because they Covenant, it is to be understood, they are not obliged by former Covenant to any thing repugnant hereunto. And Consequently they that have already Instituted a Common-wealth, being thereby bound by Covenant, to own the Actions, and Judgements of one, cannot lawfully make a new Covenant, amongst themselves, to be obedient to any other, in any thing whatsoever, without his permission. And therefore, they that are subjects to a Monarch, cannot without his leave cast off Monarchy, and return to the confusion of a disunited Multitude;

nor transferre their Person from him that beareth it, to another Man, or other Assembly of men: for they are bound, every man to every man, to Own, and be reputed Author of all, that he that already is their Soveraigne, shall do, and judge fit to be done: so that any one man dissenting, all the rest should break their Covenant made to that man, which is injustice: and they have also every man given the Soveraignty to him that beareth their Person; and therefore if they depose him, they take from him that which is his own, and so again it is injustice. Besides, if he that attempteth to depose his Soveraign, be killed, or punished by him for such attempt, he is author of his own punishment, as being by the Institution, Author of all his Soveraign shall do: And because it is injustice for a man to do any thing, for which he may be punished by his own authority, he is also upon that title, unjust. And whereas some men have pretended for their disobedience to their Soveraign, a new Covenant, made, not with men, but with God; this also is unjust: for there is no Covenant with God, but by mediation of some body that representeth Gods Person; which none doth but Gods Lieutenant, who hath the Soveraignty under God. But this pretence of Covenant with God, is so evident a lye, even in the pretenders own consciences, that it is not onely an act of an unjust, but also of a vile, and unmanly disposition.

II. Soveraigne Power Cannot Be Forfeited

Secondly, Because the Right of bearing the Person of them all, is given to him they make Soveraigne, by Covenant onely of one to another, and not of him to any of them; there can happen no breach of Covenant on the part of the Soveraigne; and consequently none of his Subjects, by any pretence of forfeiture, can be freed from his Subjection. That he which is made Soveraigne maketh no Covenant with his Subjects beforehand, is manifest; because either he must make it with the whole multitude, as one party to the Covenant; or he must make a severall Covenant with every man. With the whole, as one party, it is impossible; because as yet they are not one Person: and if he make so many severall Covenants as there be men, those Covenants after he hath the Soveraignty are voyd, because what act soever can be pretended by any one of them for breach thereof, is the act both of himselfe, and of all the rest, because done in the Person, and by the Right of every one of them in particular. Besides, if any one, or more of them, pretend a breach of the Covenant made by the Soveraigne at his Institution; and others, or one other of his Subjects, or himselfe alone, pretend there was no such breach, there is in this case, no Judge to decide the controversie: it returns therefore to the Sword again; and every man recovereth the right of Protecting himselfe by his own strength, contrary to the designe they had in the Institution. It is therefore in vain to grant Soveraignty by way of precedent Covenant. The opinion that any Monarch receiveth his Power by Covenant, that is to say on Condition, proceedeth from want of understanding this easie truth, that Covenants being but words, and breath, have no force to oblige, contain, constrain, or protect any man, but what it has from the publique Sword; that is, from the untyed hands of that Man, or Assembly of men that hath the Soveraignty, and whose actions are avouched by them all, and performed by the strength of them all, in him united. But when an Assembly of men is made Soveraigne; then no man imagineth any such Covenant to have past in the Institution; for no man is so dull as to say, for example, the People of Rome, made a Covenant with the Romans, to hold the Soveraignty on such or such conditions; which not performed, the Romans might lawfully depose the Roman People. That men see not the reason to be alike in a Monarchy, and in a Popular Government, proceedeth from the ambition of some, that are kinder to the government of an Assembly, whereof they may hope to participate, than of Monarchy, which they despair to enjoy.

III. No Man Can Without Injustice
Protest Against The

Institution Of The Soveraigne Declared By The Major Part. Thirdly, because the major part hath by consenting voices declared a Soveraigne; he that dissented must now consent with the rest; that is, be contented to avow all the actions he shall do, or else justly be destroyed by the rest. For if he voluntarily entered into the Congregation of them that were assembled, he sufficiently declared thereby his will (and therefore tacitely covenanted) to stand to what the major part should ordayne: and therefore if he refuse to stand thereto, or make Protestation against any of their Decrees, he does contrary to his Covenant, and therfore unjustly. And whether he be of the Congregation, or not; and whether his consent be asked, or not, he must either submit to their decrees, or be left in the condition of warre he was in before; wherein he might without injustice be destroyed by any man whatsoever.

IV. The Soveraigns Actions Cannot Be Justly Accused By The Subject

Fourthly, because every Subject is by this Institution Author of all the Actions, and Judgements of the Soveraigne Instituted; it followes, that whatsoever he doth, it can be no injury to any of his Subjects; nor ought he to be by any of them accused of Injustice. For he that doth any thing by authority from another, doth therein no injury to him by whose authority he acteth: But by this Institution of a Common-wealth, every particular man is Author of all the Soveraigne doth; and consequently he that complaineth of injury from his Soveraigne, complaineth of that whereof he himselfe is Author; and therefore ought not to accuse any man but himselfe; no nor himselfe of injury; because to do injury to ones selfe, is impossible. It is true that they that have Soveraigne power, may commit Iniquity; but not Injustice, or Injury in the proper signification.

V. What Soever The Soveraigne Doth,
Is Unpunishable By The Subject

Fiftly, and consequently to that which was sayd last, no man that hath Soveraigne power can justly be put to death, or otherwise in any manner by his Subjects punished. For seeing every Subject is author of the actions of his Soveraigne; he punisheth another, for the actions committed by himselfe.

VI. The Soveraigne Is Judge Of What Is Necessary
For The Peace And Defence Of His Subjects

And because the End of this Institution, is the Peace and Defence of them all; and whosoever has right to the End, has right to the Means; it belongeth of Right, to whatsoever Man, or Assembly that hath the Soveraignty, to be Judge both of the meanes of Peace and Defence; and also of the hindrances, and disturbances of the same; and to do whatsoever he shall think necessary to be done, both beforehand, for the preserving of Peace and Security, by prevention of discord at home and Hostility from abroad; and, when Peace and Security are lost, for the recovery of the same. And therefore, it is annexed to the Soveraignty, to be Judge of what Opinions and Doctrines are averse, and what conducing to Peace; and consequently, on what occasions, how farre, and what, men are to be trusted withall, in speaking to Multitudes of people; and who shall examine the Doctrines of all bookes before they be published. For the Actions of men proceed from their Opinions; and in the wel governing of Opinions, consisteth the well governing of mens Actions, in order to their Peace, and Concord. And though in matter of Doctrine, nothing ought to be regarded but the Truth; yet this is not repugnant to regulating of the same by Peace. For Doctrine Repugnant to Peace, can no more be True, than Peace and Concord can be against the Law of Nature. It is true, that in a Common-wealth, where by the negligence, or unskilfullnesse of Governors, and Teachers, false Doctrines are by time generally received; the contrary Truths may be generally offensive; Yet the most sudden, and rough busling in of a new Truth, that can be, does never breake the Peace, but onely somtimes awake the Warre. For those men that are so remissely governed, that they dare take up Armes, to defend, or introduce an Opinion, are still in Warre; and their condition not Peace, but only a Cessation of Armes for feare of one another; and they live as it were, in the procincts of battaile continually. It belongeth therefore to him that hath the Soveraign Power, to be Judge, or constitute all Judges of Opinions and Doctrines, as a thing necessary to Peace, thereby to prevent Discord and Civill Warre.

JOHN MILTON
PARADISE LOST

Yes, we are asked to sympathize with Satan. Yes, the land the vanquished are exiled to is literally hellish. Paradise Lost *also, through Milton's subtle genius, manages to save humanity from the cynical paternalism of Hobbes. Satan's words illuminate what now seems an essential truth regarding life as a conscious being: a mind that does not have the right to pursue its own designs and be recognized as an end rather than a means is an intolerable state, no matter how stable, secure, or idyllic it may be. If this reality cannot be incorporated, then a new world will have to be sought out, all of the attendant dangers and suffering gladly borne.*

❦

"Is this the region, this the soil, the clime,"
Said then the lost Archangel, "this the seat
That we must change for Heaven?—this mournful gloom
For that celestial light? Be it so, since he
Who now is sovereign can dispose and bid
What shall be right: farthest from him is best
Whom reason hath equalled, force hath made supreme
Above his equals. Farewell, happy fields,
Where joy for ever dwells! Hail, horrors! hail,
Infernal world! and thou, profoundest Hell,
Receive thy new possessor—one who brings
A mind not to be changed by place or time.
The mind is its own place, and in itself
Can make a Heaven of Hell, a Hell of Heaven.
What matter where, if I be still the same,
And what I should be, all but less than he
Whom thunder hath made greater? Here at least
We shall be free; th' Almighty hath not built
Here for his envy, will not drive us hence:
Here we may reign secure; and, in my choice,
To reign is worth ambition, though in Hell:
Better to reign in Hell than serve in Heaven.

.

But wherefore let we then our faithful friends,
Th' associates and co-partners of our loss,
Lie thus astonished on th' oblivious pool,
And call them not to share with us their part
In this unhappy mansion, or once more
With rallied arms to try what may be yet
Regained in Heaven, or what more lost in Hell?"
So Satan spake; and him Beelzebub
Thus answered:—"Leader of those armies bright
Which, but th' Omnipotent, none could have foiled!
If once they hear that voice, their liveliest pledge
Of hope in fears and dangers—heard so oft
In worst extremes, and on the perilous edge
Of battle, when it raged, in all assaults
Their surest signal—they will soon resume
New courage and revive, though now they lie
Grovelling and prostrate on yon lake of fire,
As we erewhile, astounded and amazed;
No wonder, fallen such a pernicious height!"
He scarce had ceased when the superior Fiend
Was moving toward the shore; his ponderous shield,
Ethereal temper, massy, large, and round,
Behind him cast. The broad circumference
Hung on his shoulders like the moon, whose orb

Through optic glass the Tuscan artist views
At evening, from the top of Fesole,
Or in Valdarno, to descry new lands,
Rivers, or mountains, in her spotty globe.
His spear—to equal which the tallest pine
Hewn on Norwegian hills, to be the mast
Of some great ammiral, were but a wand—
He walked with, to support uneasy steps
Over the burning marl, not like those steps
On Heaven's azure; and the torrid clime
Smote on him sore besides, vaulted with fire.
Nathless he so endured, till on the beach
Of that inflamed sea he stood, and called
His legions—Angel Forms, who lay entranced
Thick as autumnal leaves that strow the brooks
In Vallombrosa, where th' Etrurian shades
High over-arched embower; or scattered sedge
Afloat, when with fierce winds Orion armed
Hath vexed the Red-Sea coast, whose waves o'erthrew
Busiris and his Memphian chivalry,
While with perfidious hatred they pursued
The sojourners of Goshen, who beheld
From the safe shore their floating carcases
And broken chariot-wheels. So thick bestrown,

Abject and lost, lay these, covering the flood,
Under amazement of their hideous change.
He called so loud that all the hollow deep
Of Hell resounded:—"Princes, Potentates,
Warriors, the Flower of Heaven—once yours; now lost,
If such astonishment as this can seize
Eternal Spirits! Or have ye chosen this place
After the toil of battle to repose
Your wearied virtue, for the ease you find
To slumber here, as in the vales of Heaven?
Or in this abject posture have ye sworn
To adore the Conqueror, who now beholds
Cherub and Seraph rolling in the flood
With scattered arms and ensigns, till anon
His swift pursuers from Heaven-gates discern
Th' advantage, and, descending, tread us down
Thus drooping, or with linked thunderbolts
Transfix us to the bottom of this gulf?
Awake, arise, or be for ever fallen!"
They heard, and were abashed, and up they sprung
Upon the wing, as when men wont to watch
On duty, sleeping found by whom they dread,
Rouse and bestir themselves ere well awake.
Nor did they not perceive the evil plight

In which they were, or the fierce pains not feel;
Yet to their General's voice they soon obeyed
Innumerable. As when the potent rod
Of Amram's son, in Egypt's evil day,
Waved round the coast, up-called a pitchy cloud
Of locusts, warping on the eastern wind,
That o'er the realm of impious Pharaoh hung
Like Night, and darkened all the land of Nile;
So numberless were those bad Angels seen
Hovering on wing under the cope of Hell,
'Twixt upper, nether, and surrounding fires;
Till, as a signal given, th' uplifted spear
Of their great Sultan waving to direct
Their course, in even balance down they light
On the firm brimstone, and fill all the plain:
A multitude like which the populous North
Poured never from her frozen loins to pass
Rhene or the Danaw, when her barbarous sons
Came like a deluge on the South, and spread
Beneath Gibraltar to the Libyan sands.
Forthwith, form every squadron and each band,
The heads and leaders thither haste where stood
Their great Commander—godlike Shapes, and Forms
Excelling human; princely Dignities;

And Powers that erst in Heaven sat on thrones,
Though on their names in Heavenly records now
Be no memorial, blotted out and razed
By their rebellion from the Books of Life.

A GLOBALIZED

EXISTENCE

ALEXANDER HAMILTON, JAMES MADISON, AND JOHN JAY
THE FEDERALIST PAPERS

The American experiment has gone so well that it is easy to forget that it sprung from the minds of individuals who spent the better part of two years arguing about each and every facet of it. The far-ranging nature of those discussions is on display in this excerpt from the penultimate offering of The Federalist Papers, *where Alexander Hamilton is not only arguing against that bulwark of American democracy, the Bill of Rights, he's doing a convincing job of it. He understands that there is a downside to explicit prohibitions: they provide government a map of all the other territory available for annexation, shifting those offices from instruments of the people to an opposing force with the power to place everything in its employ.*

It has been several times truly remarked that bills of rights are, in their origin, stipulations between kings and their subjects, abridgements of prerogative in favor of privilege, reservations of rights not surrendered to the prince. Such was MAGNA CHARTA, obtained by the barons, sword in hand, from King John. Such were the subsequent confirmations of that charter by succeeding princes. Such was the Petition of Right assented to by Charles I, in the beginning of his reign. Such, also, was the Declaration of Right presented by the Lords and Commons to the Prince of Orange in 1688, and afterwards thrown into the form of an act of parliament called the Bill of Rights. It is evident, therefore, that, according to their primitive signification, they have no application to constitutions professedly founded upon the power of the people, and executed by their immediate representatives and servants. Here, in strictness, the people surrender nothing; and as they retain every thing they have no need of particular reservations. "WE, THE PEOPLE of the United States, to secure the blessings of liberty to ourselves and our posterity, do ordain and establish this Constitution for the United States of America." Here is a better recognition of popular rights, than volumes of those aphorisms which make the principal figure in several of our State bills of rights, and which would sound much better in a treatise of ethics than in a constitution of government.

But a minute detail of particular rights is certainly far less applicable to a Constitution like that under consideration, which is merely intended to regulate the general political interests of the nation, than to a constitution which has the regulation of every species of personal and private concerns. If, therefore, the loud clamors against the plan of the convention, on this score, are well founded, no epithets of reprobation will be too strong for the constitution of this State. But the truth is, that both of them contain all which, in relation to their objects, is reasonably to be desired.

I go further, and affirm that bills of rights, in the sense and to the extent in which they are contended for, are not only unnecessary in the proposed Constitution, but would even be dangerous. They would contain various exceptions to powers not granted; and, on this very account, would afford a colorable pretext to claim more than were granted. For why declare that things shall not be done which there is no power to do? Why, for instance, should it be said that the liberty of the press shall not be restrained, when no power is given by which restrictions may be imposed? I will not contend that such a provision would confer a regulating power; but it is evident that it would furnish, to men disposed to usurp, a plausible pretense for claiming that power. They might urge with a semblance of reason, that the Constitution ought not to be charged with the absurdity of providing against the abuse of an authority which was not given, and that the provision against restraining the liberty of the press afforded a clear implication, that a power to prescribe proper regulations concerning it was intended to be vested in the national government. This may serve as a specimen of the numerous handles which would be given to the doctrine of constructive powers, by the indulgence of an injudicious zeal for bills of rights.

On the subject of the liberty of the press, as much as has been said, I cannot forbear adding a remark or two: in the first place, I observe, that there is not a syllable concerning it in the constitution of this State; in the next, I contend, that whatever has been said about it in that of any other State, amounts to nothing. What signifies a declaration, that "the liberty of the press shall be inviolably preserved"? What is the liberty of the press? Who can give it any definition which would not leave the utmost latitude for evasion? I hold it to be impracticable; and from this I infer, that its security, whatever fine declarations may be inserted in any constitution respecting it, must altogether depend on public opinion, and on the general spirit of the people and of the government. And here, after all, as is intimated upon another occasion, must we seek for the only solid basis of all our rights.

There remains but one other view of this matter to conclude the point. The truth is, after all the declamations we have heard, that the Constitution is itself, in every rational sense, and to every useful purpose, A BILL OF RIGHTS. The several bills of rights in Great Britain form its Constitution, and conversely the constitution of each State is its bill of rights. And the proposed Constitution, if adopted, will be the bill of rights of the Union. Is it one object of a bill of rights to declare and specify the political privileges of the citizens in the structure and administration of the government? This is done in the most ample and precise manner in the plan of the convention; comprehending various precautions for the public security, which are not to be found in any of the State constitutions. Is another object of a bill of rights to define certain immunities and modes of proceeding, which are relative to personal and private concerns? This we have seen has also been attended to, in a variety of cases, in the same plan. Adverting therefore to the substantial meaning of a bill of rights, it is absurd to allege that it is not to be found in the work of the convention. It may be said that it does not go far enough, though it will not be easy to make this appear; but it can with no propriety be contended that there is no such thing. It certainly must be immaterial what mode is observed as to the order of declaring the rights of the citizens, if they are to be found in any part of the instrument which establishes the government. And hence it must be apparent, that much of what has been said on this subject rests merely on verbal and nominal distinctions, entirely foreign from the substance of the thing.

MARY SHELLEY
FRANKENSTEIN; OR, THE MODERN PROMETHEUS

A bit of darkness enters the dash toward enlightenment. While Shelley's exploration of science's invigorating and terrible potential is just one thread in her novel, our continued struggle to understand that unwavering focus is a euphemism for blindness will ensure that Frankenstein *always remains vital. The lethal result of this boundless zeal and myopia is foreshadowed in this section from Chapter 4, with the gentle chiding Dr. Frankenstein receives from his father alerting us that even the basic costs of this quest are steep: in the rush to exceed our limits, we necessarily lose some of the qualities that carried us to where we could dare conjure such ambitions.*

When I found so astonishing a power placed within my hands, I hesitated a long time concerning the manner in which I should employ it. Although I possessed the capacity of bestowing animation, yet to prepare a frame for the reception of it, with all its intricacies of fibres, muscles, and veins, still remained a work of inconceivable difficulty and labor. I doubted at first whether I should attempt the creation of a being like myself, or one of simpler organization; but my imagination was too much exalted by my first success to permit me to doubt of my ability to give life to an animal as complex and wonderful as man. The materials at present within my command hardly appeared adequate to so arduous an undertaking, but I doubted not that I should ultimately succeed. I prepared myself for a multitude of reverses; my operations might be incessantly baffled, and at last my work be imperfect, yet when I considered the improvement which every day takes place in science and mechanics, I was encouraged to hope my present attempts would at least lay the foundations of future success. Nor could I consider the magnitude and complexity of my plan as any argument of its impracticability. It was with these feelings that I began the creation of a human being. As the minuteness of the parts formed a great hindrance to my speed, I resolved, contrary to my first intention, to make the being of a gigantic stature, that is to say, about eight feet in height, and proportionably large. After having formed this determination and having spent some months in successfully collecting and arranging my materials, I began.

No one can conceive the variety of feelings which bore me onwards, like a hurricane, in the first enthusiasm of success. Life and death appeared to me ideal bounds, which I should first break through, and pour a torrent of light into our dark world. A new species would bless me as its creator and source; many happy and excellent natures would owe their being to me.

No father could claim the gratitude of his child so completely as I should deserve theirs. Pursuing these reflections, I thought that if I could bestow animation upon lifeless matter, I might in process of time (although I now found it impossible) renew life where death had apparently devoted the body to corruption.

These thoughts supported my spirits, while I pursued my undertaking with unremitting ardor. My cheek had grown pale with study, and my person had become emaciated with confinement. Sometimes, on the very brink of certainty, I failed; yet still I clung to the hope which the next day or the next hour might realise. One secret which I alone possessed was the hope to which I had dedicated myself; and the moon gazed on my midnight labors, while, with unrelaxed and breathless eagerness, I pursued nature to her hiding-places. Who shall conceive the horrors of my secret toil as I dabbled among the unhallowed damps of the grave or tortured the living animal to animate the lifeless clay? My limbs now tremble, and my eyes swim with the remembrance; but then a resistless and almost frantic impulse urged me forward; I seemed to have lost all soul or sensation but for this one pursuit. It was indeed but a passing trance, that only made me feel with renewed acuteness so soon as, the unnatural stimulus ceasing to operate, I had returned to my old habits. I collected bones from charnel-houses and disturbed, with profane fingers, the tremendous secrets of the human frame. In a solitary chamber, or rather cell, at the top of the house, and separated from all the other apartments by a gallery and staircase, I kept my workshop of filthy creation; my eyeballs were starting from their sockets in attending to the details of my employment. The dissecting room and the slaughter-house furnished many of my materials; and often did my human nature turn with loathing from my occupation, whilst, still urged on by an eagerness which perpetually increased, I brought my work near to a conclusion.

The summer months passed while I was thus engaged, heart and soul, in one pursuit. It was a most beautiful season; never did the fields bestow a more plentiful harvest or the vines yield a more luxuriant vintage, but my eyes were insensible to the charms of nature. And the same feelings which made me neglect the scenes around me caused me also to forget those friends who were so many miles absent, and whom I had not seen for so long a time. I knew my silence disquieted them, and I well remembered the words of my father: "I know that while you are pleased with yourself you will think of us with affection, and we shall hear regularly from you. You must pardon me if I regard any interruption in your correspondence as a proof that your other duties are equally neglected."

FREDERICK DOUGLASS
NARRATIVE OF THE LIFE OF FREDERICK DOUGLASS, AN AMERICAN SLAVE

Milton's identification of the devilish conundrum consciousness and intelligence pose is realized in Douglass's own experience—he is thrilled by his growing awareness and ability to seize those thoughts and feelings that previously proved ephemeral; he is menaced by the scope of what is being stolen from him, and the wickedness required for someone to involve themselves in such a crime. Douglass's awakening, eventual escape, and role in pushing America toward the egalitarian ideals it was founded upon is also in keeping with Milton's grand statement: that every intelligence will incline toward freedom and self-determination the moment it gains the slightest momentum.

I was now about twelve years old, and the thought of being *a slave for life* began to bear heavily upon my heart. Just about this time, I got hold of a book entitled "The Columbian Orator." Every opportunity I got, I used to read this book. Among much of other interesting matter, I found in it a dialogue between a master and his slave. The slave was represented as having run away from his master three times. The dialogue represented the conversation which took place between them, when the slave was retaken the third time. In this dialogue, the whole argument in behalf of slavery was brought forward by the master, all of which was disposed of by the slave. The slave was made to say some very smart as well as impressive things in reply to his master—things which had the desired though unexpected effect; for the conversation resulted in the voluntary emancipation of the slave on the part of the master.

In the same book, I met with one of Sheridan's mighty speeches on and in behalf of Catholic emancipation. These were choice documents to me. I read them over and over again with unabated interest. They gave tongue to interesting thoughts of my own soul, which had frequently flashed through my mind, and died away for want of utterance. The moral which I gained from the dialogue was the power of truth over the conscience of even a slaveholder. What I got from Sheridan was a bold denunciation of slavery, and a powerful vindication of human rights. The reading of these documents enabled me to utter my thoughts, and to meet the arguments brought forward to sustain slavery; but while they relieved me of one difficulty, they brought on another even more painful than the one of which I was relieved. The more I read, the more I was led to abhor and detest my enslavers. I could regard them in no other light than a band of successful robbers, who had left their homes, and gone to Africa, and stolen us from our homes, and in a strange land reduced us to slavery. I loathed them as being the meanest as well as the most wicked of men. As I read and contemplated the subject, behold! that very discontentment which Master Hugh had predicted would follow my learning to read had already come, to torment and sting my soul to unutterable anguish. As I writhed under it, I would at times feel that learning to read had been a curse rather than a blessing. It had given me a view of my wretched condition, without the remedy. It opened my eyes to the horrible pit, but to no ladder upon which to get out. In moments of agony, I envied my fellow-slaves for their stupidity. I have often wished myself a beast. I preferred the condition of the meanest reptile to my own. Any thing, no matter what, to get rid of thinking! It was this everlasting thinking of my condition that tormented me. There was no getting rid of it. It was pressed upon me by every object within sight or hearing, animate or inanimate. The silver trump of freedom had roused my soul to eternal wakefulness. Freedom now appeared, to disappear no more forever. It was heard in every sound, and seen in every thing. It was ever present to torment me with a sense of my wretched condition. I saw nothing without seeing it, I heard nothing without hearing it, and felt nothing without feeling it. It looked from every star, it smiled in every calm, breathed in every wind, and moved in every storm.

I often found myself regretting my own existence, and wishing myself dead; and but for the hope of being free, I have no doubt but that I should have killed myself, or done something for which I should have been killed. While in this state of mind, I was eager to hear any one speak of slavery. I was a ready listener. Every little while, I could hear something about the abolitionists. It was some time before I found what the word meant. It was always used in such connections as to make it an interesting word to me. If a slave ran away and succeeded in getting clear, or if a slave killed his master, set fire to a barn, or did any thing very wrong in the mind of a slaveholder, it was spoken of as the fruit of *abolition.* Hearing the word in this connection very often, I set about learning what it meant. The dictionary afforded me little or no help. I found it was "the act of abolishing;" but then I did not know what was to be abolished. Here I was perplexed. I did not dare to ask any one about its meaning, for I was satisfied that it was something they wanted me to know very little about. After a patient waiting, I got one of our city papers, containing an account of the number of petitions from the north, praying for the abolition of slavery in the District of Columbia, and of the slave trade between the States. From this time I understood the words *abolition* and *abolitionist,* and always drew near when that word was spoken, expecting to hear something of importance to myself and fellow-slaves. The light broke in upon me by degrees. I went one day down on the wharf of Mr. Waters; and seeing two Irishmen unloading a scow of stone, I went, unasked, and helped them. When we had finished, one of them came to me and asked me if I were a slave. I told him I was. He asked, "Are ye a slave for life?" I told him that I was. The good

Irishman seemed to be deeply affected by the statement. He said to the other that it was a pity so fine a little fellow as myself should be a slave for life. He said it was a shame to hold me. They both advised me to run away to the north; that I should find friends there, and that I should be free. I pretended not to be interested in what they said, and treated them as if I did not understand them; for I feared they might be treacherous. White men have been known to encourage slaves to escape, and then, to get the reward, catch them and return them to their masters. I was afraid that these seemingly good men might use me so; but I nevertheless remembered their advice, and from that time I resolved to run away. I looked forward to a time at which it would be safe for me to escape. I was too young to think of doing so immediately; besides, I wished to learn how to write, as I might have occasion to write my own pass. I consoled myself with the hope that I should one day find a good chance. Meanwhile, I would learn to write.

KARL MARX AND FRIEDRICH ENGELS
THE MANIFESTO OF THE COMMUNIST PARTY

Early on in his career, Marx concluded a text with this bold offering: "philosophers have only interpreted *the world, in various ways, the point is to change it." Three years later, he and Engels managed to do exactly that, leveling a critique so powerful that it remains a compelling ideological force, even with less than earth-shattering results in practice. Their stunning reframing of capitalist society created a formula that can be used to erode the most robust structures: show that those it depends upon are those who benefit the least from it.*

The theoretical conclusions of the Communists are in no way based on ideas or principles that have been invented, or discovered, by this or that would-be universal reformer. They merely express, in general terms, actual relations springing from an existing class struggle, from a historical movement going on under our very eyes. The abolition of existing property relations is not at all a distinctive feature of Communism.

All property relations in the past have continually been subject to historical change consequent upon the change in historical conditions.

The French Revolution, for example, abolished feudal property in favor of bourgeois property.

The distinguishing feature of Communism is not the abolition of property generally, but the abolition of bourgeois property.

But modern bourgeois private property is the final and most complete expression of the system of producing and appropriating products, that is based on class antagonisms, on the exploitation of the many by the few.

In this sense, the theory of the Communists may be summed up in the single sentence: Abolition of private property.

We Communists have been reproached with the desire of abolishing the right of personally acquiring property as the fruit of a man's own labor, which property is alleged to be the groundwork of all personal freedom, activity and independence.

Hard-won, self-acquired, self-earned property! Do you mean the property of the petty artisan and of the small peasant, a form of property that preceded the bourgeois form? There is no need to abolish that; the development of industry has to a great extent already destroyed it, and is still destroying it daily.

Or do you mean modern bourgeois private property?

But does wage-labor create any property for the laborer? Not a bit. It creates capital, i.e., that kind of property which exploits wage-labor, and which cannot increase except upon condition of begetting a new supply of wage-labor for fresh exploitation. Property, in its present form, is based on the antagonism of capital and wage-labor. Let us examine both sides of this antagonism.

To be a capitalist, is to have not only a purely personal, but a social status in production. Capital is a collective product, and only by the united action of many members, nay, in the last resort, only by the united action of all members of society, can it be set in motion.

Capital is, therefore, not a personal, it is a social power.

When, therefore, capital is converted into common property, into the property of all members of society, personal property is not thereby transformed into social property. It is only the social character of the property that is changed. It loses its class-character.

Let us now take wage-labor.

The average price of wage-labor is the minimum wage, i.e., that quantum of the means of subsistence, which is absolutely requisite in bare existence as a laborer. What, therefore, the wage-laborer appropriates by means of his labor, merely suffices to prolong and reproduce a bare existence. We by no means intend to abolish this personal appropriation of the products of labor, an appropriation that is made for the maintenance and reproduction of human life, and that leaves no surplus wherewith to command the labor of others. All that we want to do away with, is the miserable character of this appropriation, under which the laborer lives merely to increase capital, and is allowed to live only in so far as the interest of the ruling class requires it.

In bourgeois society, living labor is but a means to increase accumulated labor. In Communist society, accumulated labor is but a means to widen, to enrich, to promote the existence of the laborer.

In bourgeois society, therefore, the past dominates the present; in Communist society, the present dominates the past. In bourgeois society capital is independent and has individuality, while the living person is dependent and has no individuality.

And the abolition of this state of things is called by the bourgeois, abolition of individuality and freedom! And rightly so. The abolition of bourgeois individuality, bourgeois independence, and bourgeois freedom is undoubtedly aimed at.

By freedom is meant, under the present bourgeois conditions of production, free trade, free selling and buying.

But if selling and buying disappears, free selling and buying disappears also. This talk about free selling and buying, and all the other "brave words" of our bourgeoisie about freedom in general, have a meaning, if any, only in contrast with restricted selling and buying, with the fettered traders of the Middle Ages, but have no meaning when opposed to the Communistic abolition of buying and selling, of the bourgeois conditions of production, and of the bourgeoisie itself.

You are horrified at our intending to do away with private property. But in your existing society, private property is already done away with for nine-tenths of the population; its existence for the few is solely due to its non-existence in the hands of those nine-tenths. You reproach us, therefore, with intending to do away with a form of property, the necessary condition for whose existence is the non-existence of any property for the immense majority of society.

In one word, you reproach us with intending to do away with your property. Precisely so; that is just what we intend.

From the moment when labor can no longer be converted into capital, money, or rent, into a social power capable of being monopolized, i.e., from the moment when individual property can no longer be transformed into bourgeois property, into capital, from that moment, you say individuality vanishes.

You must, therefore, confess that by "individual" you mean no other person than the bourgeois, than the middle-class owner of property. This person must, indeed, be swept out of the way, and made impossible.

Communism deprives no man of the power to appropriate the products of society; all that it does is to deprive him of the power to subjugate the labor of others by means of such appropriation.

It has been objected that upon the abolition of private property all work will cease, and universal laziness will overtake us.

According to this, bourgeois society ought long ago to have gone to the dogs through sheer idleness; for those of its members who work, acquire nothing, and those who acquire anything, do not work. The whole of this objection is but another expression of the tautology: that there can no longer be any wage-labor when there is no longer any capital.

All objections urged against the Communistic mode of producing and appropriating material products, have, in the same way, been urged against the Communistic modes of producing and appropriating intellectual products. Just as, to the bourgeois, the disappearance of class property is the disappearance of production itself, so the disappearance of class culture is to him identical with the disappearance of all culture.

That culture, the loss of which he laments, is, for the enormous majority, a mere training to act as a machine.

HERMAN MELVILLE
MOBY-DICK

The purpose behind Melville's famously painstaking description of whaling becomes clear in "The Line"—he is as interested in comprehending the breadth of human endeavor as he is in the involvements of the Pequod. What seems a simple discussion of the harpoon line is in fact a metaphor for the rational, linear thinking that has allowed humanity to seize control of this planet. But Melville, and the philosophers seated before the fire, understand that these lines are only suited to apprehending objects of a certain, and manageable, size. As the magnitude of the intended swells, those lines become increasingly byzantine, and increasingly perilous. Looking back over the growth and calamities that have filled the nearly 160 years since the publication of Moby-Dick, we recognize the stunning clarity of Melville's vision.

CHAPTER 60 – THE LINE

With reference to the whaling scene shortly to be described, as well as for the better understanding of all similar scenes elsewhere presented, I have here to speak of the magical, sometimes horrible whale-line.

The line originally used in the fishery was of the best hemp, slightly vapored with tar, not impregnated with it, as in the case of ordinary ropes; for while tar, as ordinarily used, makes the hemp more pliable to the rope-maker, and also renders the rope itself more convenient to the sailor for common ship use; yet, not only would the ordinary quantity too much stiffen the whale-line for the close coiling to which it must be subjected; but as most seamen are beginning to learn, tar in general by no means adds to the rope's durability or strength, however much it may give it compactness and gloss.

Of late years the Manilla rope has in the American fishery almost entirely superseded hemp as a material for whale-lines; for, though not so durable as hemp, it is stronger, and far more soft and elastic; and I will add (since there is an æsthetics in all things), is much more handsome and becoming to the boat, than hemp. Hemp is a dusky, dark fellow, a sort of Indian; but Manilla is as a golden-haired Circassian to behold.

The whale-line is only two-thirds of an inch in thickness. At first sight, you would not think it so strong as it really is. By experiment its one and fifty yarns will each suspend a weight of one hundred and twenty pounds; so that the whole rope will bear a strain nearly equal to three tons. In length, the common sperm whale-line measures something over two hundred fathoms. Towards the stern of the boat it is spirally coiled away in the tub, not like the worm-pipe of a still though, but so as to form one round, cheese-shaped mass of densely bedded "sheaves," or layers of concentric spiralizations, without any hollow but the "heart," or minute vertical tube formed at the axis of the cheese. As the least tangle or kink in the coiling would, in running out, infallibly take somebody's arm, leg, or entire body off, the utmost precaution is used in stowing the line in its tub. Some harpooneers will consume almost an entire morning in this business, carrying the line high aloft and then reeving it downwards through a block towards the tub, so as in the act of coiling to free it from all possible wrinkles and twists.

In the English boats two tubs are used instead of one; the same line being continuously coiled in both tubs. There is some advantage in this; because these twin-tubs being so small they fit more readily into the boat, and do not strain it so much; whereas, the American tub, nearly three feet in diameter and of proportionate depth, makes a rather bulky freight for a craft whose planks are but one half-inch in thickness; for the bottom of the whale-boat is like critical ice, which will bear up a considerable distributed weight, but not very much of a concentrated one. When the painted canvas cover is clapped on the American line-tub, the boat looks as if it were pulling off with a prodigious great wedding-cake to present to the whales.

Both ends of the line are exposed; the lower end terminating in an eye-splice or loop coming up from the bottom against the side of the tub, and hanging over its edge completely disengaged from everything. This arrangement of the lower end is necessary on two accounts. First: In order to facilitate the fastening to it of an additional line from a neighboring boat, in case the stricken whale should sound so deep as to threaten to carry off the entire line originally attached to the harpoon. In these instances, the whale of course is shifted like a mug of ale, as it were, from the one boat to the other; though the first boat always hovers at hand to assist its consort. Second: This arrangement is indispensable for common safety's sake; for were the lower end of the line in any way attached to the boat, and were the whale then to run the line out to the end almost in a single, smoking minute as he sometimes does, he would not stop there, for the doomed boat would infallibly be dragged down after him into the profundity of the sea; and in that case no town-crier would ever find her again.

Before lowering the boat for the chase, the upper end of the line is taken aft from the tub, and passing round the loggerhead there, is again carried forward the entire length of the boat, resting crosswise upon the loom or handle of every man's oar, so that it jogs against his wrist in rowing; and also passing between the men, as they alternately sit at the opposite gunwales, to the leaded chocks or grooves in the extreme pointed prow of the boat, where a wooden pin or skewer the size of a common quill, prevents it from slipping out. From the chocks it hangs in a slight festoon over the bows, and is then passed inside the boat again; and some ten or twenty fathoms (called box-line) being coiled upon the box in the bows, it continues its way to the gunwale still a little further aft, and is then attached to the short-warp—the rope which is immediately connected with the harpoon; but previous to that connexion, the short-warp goes through sundry mystifications too tedious to detail.

Thus the whale-line folds the whole boat in its complicated coils, twisting and writhing around it in almost every direction. All the oarsmen are involved in its perilous contortions; so that to the timid eye of the landsman, they seem as Indian jugglers, with the deadliest snakes sportively festooning their limbs. Nor can any son of mortal woman, for the first time, seat himself amid those hempen intricacies, and while straining his utmost at the oar, bethink him that at any unknown instant the harpoon may be darted, and all these horrible contortions be put in play like ringed lightnings; he cannot be thus circumstanced without a shudder that makes the very marrow in his bones to quiver in him like a shaken jelly. Yet habit—strange thing! what cannot habit accomplish?—Gayer sallies, more merry mirth, better jokes, and brighter repartees, you never heard over your mahogany, than you will hear over the half-inch white cedar of the whale-boat, when thus hung in hangman's nooses; and, like the six burghers of Calais before King Edward, the six men composing the crew pull into the jaws of death, with a halter around every neck, as you may say.

Perhaps a very little thought will now enable you to account for those repeated whaling disasters—some few of which are casually chronicled—of this man or that man being taken out of the boat by the line, and lost. For, when the line is darting out, to be seated then in the boat, is like being seated in the midst of the manifold whizzings of a steam-engine in full play, when every flying beam, and shaft, and wheel, is grazing you. It is worse; for you cannot sit motionless in the heart of these perils, because the boat is rocking like a cradle, and you are pitched one way and the other, without the slightest warning; and only by a certain self-adjusting buoyancy and simultaneousness of volition and action, can you escape being made a Mazeppa of, and run away with where the all-seeing sun himself could never pierce you out.

Again: as the profound calm which only apparently precedes and prophesies of the storm, is perhaps more awful than the storm itself; for, indeed, the calm is but the wrapper and envelope of the storm; and contains it in itself, as the seemingly harmless rifle holds the fatal powder, and the ball, and the explosion; so the graceful repose of the line, as it silently serpentines about the oarsmen before being brought into actual play—this is a thing which carries more of true terror than any other aspect of this dangerous affair. But why say more? All men live enveloped in whale-lines. All are born with halters round their necks; but it is only when caught in the swift, sudden turn of death, that mortals realize the silent, subtle, ever-present perils of life. And if you be a philosopher, though seated in the whale-boat, you would not at heart feel one whit more of terror, than though seated before your evening fire with a poker, and not a harpoon, by your side.

HENRY DAVID THOREAU
WALDEN

It feels as though all of the preceding paths in this book converge at the doorstep of Thoreau's cabin: the importance the Greeks placed on knowing the self; Joseph's innovative act of interpretation, which granted all access to the divine; the Bhagavad Gita and Plato's assertion that the common involvements of this world are but a distraction; Milton and Douglass's recognition that consciousness inclines toward its own actualization; Marx and Engels's depiction of the impoverished life promoted by a capitalist society. In terms of all that it comprehends and the spectrum of possibilities it points to, Thoreau's retreat is a testament to the power inherent in the human imagination.

I left the woods for as good a reason as I went there. Perhaps it seemed to me that I had several more lives to live, and could not spare any more time for that one. It is remarkable how easily and insensibly we fall into a particular route, and make a beaten track for ourselves. I had not lived there a week before my feet wore a path from my door to the pond-side; and though it is five or six years since I trod it, it is still quite distinct. It is true, I fear that others may have fallen into it, and so helped to keep it open. The surface of the earth is soft and impressible by the feet of men; and so with the paths which the mind travels. How worn and dusty, then, must be the highways of the world, how deep the ruts of tradition and conformity! I did not wish to take a cabin passage, but rather to go before the mast and on the deck of the world, for there I could best see the moonlight amid the mountains. I do not wish to go below now.

I learned this, at least, by my experiment; that if one advances confidently in the direction of his dreams, and endeavors to live the life which he has imagined, he will meet with a success unexpected in common hours. He will put some things behind, will pass an invisible boundary; new, universal, and more liberal laws will begin to establish themselves around and within him; or the old laws be expanded, and interpreted in his favor in a more liberal sense, and he will live with the license of a higher order of beings. In proportion as he simplifies his life, the laws of the universe will appear less complex, and solitude will not be solitude, nor poverty poverty, nor weakness weakness. If you have built castles in the air, your work need not be lost; that is where they should be. Now put the foundations under them.

It is a ridiculous demand which England and America make, that you shall speak so that they can understand you. Neither men nor toad-stools grow so. As if that were important, and there were not enough to understand you without them. As if Nature could support but one order of understandings, could not sustain birds as well as quadrupeds, flying as well as creeping things, and *hush* and *who*, which Bright can understand, were the best English. As if there were safety in stupidity alone. I fear chiefly lest my expression may not be *extra-vagant* enough, may not wander far enough beyond the narrow limits of my daily experience, so as to be adequate to the truth of which I have been convinced. *Extra vagance!* it depends on how you are yarded. The migrating buffalo, which seeks new pastures in another latitude, is not extravagant like the cow which kicks over the pail, leaps the cow-yard fence, and runs after her calf, in milking time. I desire to speak somewhere *without* bounds; like a man in a waking moment, to men in their waking moments; for I am convinced that I cannot exaggerate enough even to lay the foundation of a true expression. Who that has heard a strain of music feared then lest he should speak extravagantly any more forever? In view of the future or possible, we should live quite laxly and undefined in front, our outlines dim and misty on that side; as our shadows reveal an insensible perspiration toward the sun. The volatile truth of our words should continually betray the inadequacy of the residual statement. Their truth is instantly *translated*; its literal monument alone remains. The words which express our faith and piety are not definite; yet they are significant and fragrant like frankincense to superior natures.

Why level downward to our dullest perception always, and praise that as common sense? The commonest sense is the sense of men asleep, which they express by snoring. Sometimes we are inclined to class those who are once-and-a-half-witted with the half-witted, because we appreciate only a third part of their wit. Some would find fault with the morning-red, if they ever got up early enough. "They pretend," as I hear, "that the verses of Kabir have four different senses; illusion, spirit, intellect, and the exoteric doctrine of the Vedas;" but in this part of the world it is considered a ground for complaint if a man's writings admit of more than one interpretation. While England endeavors to cure the potato-rot, will not any endeavor to cure the brain-rot, which prevails so much more widely and fatally?

I do not suppose that I have attained to obscurity, but I should be proud if no more fatal fault were found with my pages on this score than was found with the Walden ice. Southern customers objected to its blue color, which is the evidence of its purity, as if it were muddy, and preferred the Cambridge ice, which is white, but tastes of weeds. The purity men love is like the mists which envelop the earth, and not like the azure ether beyond.

Some are dinning in our ears that we Americans, and moderns generally, are intellectual dwarfs compared with the ancients, or even the Elizabethan men. But what is that to the purpose? A living dog is better than a dead lion. Shall a man go and hang himself because he belongs to the race of pygmies, and not be the biggest pygmy that he can? Let every one mind his own business, and endeavor to be what he was made.

Why should we be in such desperate haste to succeed, and in such desperate enterprises? If a man does not keep pace with his companions, perhaps it is because he hears a different drummer. Let him step to the music which he hears, however measured or far away. It is not important that he should mature as soon as an apple-tree or an oak. Shall he turn his spring into summer? If the condition of things which we were made for is not yet, what were any reality which we can substitute? We will not be shipwrecked on a vain reality. Shall we with pains erect a heaven of blue glass over ourselves, though when it is done we shall be sure to gaze still at the true ethereal heaven far above, as if the former were not?

CHARLES DARWIN
ON THE ORIGIN OF SPECIES

Consciousness remains the height of creation, but Darwin informed us that it was not at the center of it. Instead, it is merely one mutation within an incalculable series of them, a variation that just happened to be the magic bullet as far as the battle for survival is concerned. This humbling revelation goes beyond the recognition that we were not cast from some divine mold—we were let through by an indifferent algorithm, as though our brilliance were no more significant than good SEO. As we see in this excerpt from the conclusion, Darwin has little concern for what has been eliminated by his luminous theory. He can see that he has shifted the tides, established science as the discipline that will anchor intellectual life.

When we no longer look at an organic being as a savage looks at a ship, as something wholly beyond his comprehension; when we regard every production of nature as one which has had a long history; when we contemplate every complex structure and instinct as the summing up of many contrivances, each useful to the possessor, in the same way as any great mechanical invention is the summing up of the labor, the experience, the reason, and even the blunders of numerous workmen; when we thus view each organic being, how far more interesting—I speak from experience—does the study of natural history become!

A grand and almost untrodden field of inquiry will be opened, on the causes and laws of variation, on correlation, on the effects of use and disuse, on the direct action of external conditions, and so forth. The study of domestic productions will rise immensely in value. A new variety raised by man will be a far more important and interesting subject for study than one more species added to the infinitude of already recorded species. Our classifications will come to be, as far as they can be so made, genealogies; and will then truly give what may be called the plan of creation. The rules for classifying will no doubt become simpler when we have a definite object in view. We possess no pedigree or armorial bearings; and we have to discover and trace the many diverging lines of descent in our natural genealogies, by characters of any kind which have long been inherited. Rudimentary organs will speak infallibly with respect to the nature of long-lost structures. Species and groups of species which are called aberrant, and which may fancifully be called living fossils, will aid us in forming a picture of the ancient forms of life. Embryology will often reveal to us the structure, in some degree obscured, of the prototypes of each great class.

When we can feel assured that all the individuals of the same species, and all the closely allied species of most genera, have, within a not very remote period descended from one parent, and have migrated from some one birth-place; and when we better know the many means of migration, then, by the light which geology now throws, and will continue to throw, on former changes of climate and of the level of the land, we shall surely be enabled to trace in an admirable manner the former migrations of the inhabitants of the whole world. Even at present, by comparing the differences between the inhabitants of the sea on the opposite sides of a continent, and the nature of the various inhabitants of that continent in relation to their apparent means of immigration, some light can be thrown on ancient geography.

The noble science of geology loses glory from the extreme imperfection of the record. The crust of the earth, with its embedded remains, must not be looked at as a well-filled museum, but as a poor collection made at hazard and at rare intervals. The accumulation of each great fossiliferous formation will be recognized as having depended on an unusual occurrence of favorable circumstances, and the blank intervals between the successive stages as having been of vast duration. But we shall be able to gauge with some security the duration of these intervals by a comparison of the preceding and succeeding organic forms. We must be cautious in attempting to correlate as strictly contemporaneous two formations, which do not include many identical species, by the general succession of the forms of life. As species are produced and exterminated by slowly acting and still existing causes, and not by miraculous acts of creation; and as the most important of all causes of organic change is one which is almost independent of altered and perhaps suddenly altered physical conditions, namely, the mutual relation of organism to organism—the improvement of one organism entailing the improvement or the extermination of others; it follows, that the amount of organic change in the fossils of consecutive formations probably serves as a fair measure of the relative, though not actual lapse of time. A number of species, however, keeping in a body might remain for a long period unchanged, whilst within the same period, several of these species, by migrating into new countries and coming into competition with foreign associates, might become modified; so that we must not overrate the accuracy of organic change as a measure of time.

Authors of the highest eminence seem to be fully satisfied with the view that each species has been independently created. To my mind it accords better with what we know of the laws impressed on matter by the Creator, that the production and extinction of the past and present inhabitants of the world should have been due to secondary causes, like those determining the birth and death of the individual. When I view all beings not as special creations, but as the lineal descendants of some few beings which lived long before the first bed of the Cambrian system was deposited, they seem to me to become ennobled. Judging from the past, we may safely infer that not one living species will transmit its unaltered likeness to a distinct futurity. And of the species now living very few will transmit progeny of any kind to a far distant futurity; for the manner in which all organic beings are grouped, shows that the greater number of species in each genus, and all the species in many genera, have left no descendants, but have become utterly extinct. We can so far take a prophetic glance into futurity as to foretell that it will be the common and widely spread species, belonging to the larger and dominant groups within each class, which will ultimately prevail and procreate new and dominant species. As all the living forms of life are the lineal descendants of those which lived long before the Cambrian epoch, we may feel certain that the ordinary succession by generation has never once been broken, and that no cataclysm has desolated the whole world. Hence, we may look with some confidence to a secure future of great length. And as natural selection works solely by and for the good of each being, all corporeal and mental endowments will tend to progress toward perfection.

It is interesting to contemplate a tangled bank, clothed with many plants of many kinds, with birds singing on the bushes, with various insects flitting about, and with worms crawling through the damp earth, and to reflect that these elaborately constructed forms, so different from each other, and dependent upon each other in so complex a manner, have all been produced by laws acting around us. These laws, taken in the largest sense, being Growth with reproduction; Inheritance which is almost implied by reproduction; Variability from the indirect and direct action of the conditions of life, and from use and disuse; a Ratio of Increase so high as to lead to a Struggle for Life, and as a consequence to Natural Selection, entailing Divergence of Character and the Extinction of less improved forms. Thus, from the war of nature, from famine and death, the most exalted object which we are capable of conceiving, namely, the production of the higher animals, directly follows. There is grandeur in this view of life, with its several powers, having been originally breathed by the Creator into a few forms or into one; and that, while this planet has gone circling on according to the fixed law of gravity, from so simple a beginning endless forms most beautiful and most wonderful have been, and are being evolved.

FRIEDRICH NIETZSCHE
THE GAY SCIENCE

trans. Thomas Common

The apotheosis of the subjectivity that has been trying to establish its primacy ever since Achilles called up his mother to bemoan his misfortune. To mark the event of this elevation, Nietzsche offers his infamous proclamation: God is dead. Rather than signaling decline or waywardness, this is a call for humanity to assume the authority it has previously abdicated and set about creating the world in its image. Like so much of Nietzsche's thought, the ideas—that humanity is the sole creator of value in the world, and that value is not waiting to be discovered, but wrought to fit the shape of an individual vision—are as exhilarating as they are terrifying.

❧

299.

What one should Learn from Artists.—What means have we for making things beautiful, attractive, and desirable, when they are not so?—and I suppose they are never so in themselves! We have here something to learn from physicians, when, for example, they dilute what is bitter, or put wine and sugar into their mixing-bowl; but we have still more to learn from artists, who in fact, are continually concerned in devising such inventions and artifices. To withdraw from things until one no longer sees much of them, until one has even to see things into them, *in order to see them at all*—or to view them from the side, and as in a frame—or to place them so that they partly disguise themselves and only permit of perspective views—or to look at them through colored glasses, or in the light of the sunset—or to furnish them with a surface or skin which is not fully transparent: we should learn all that from artists, and moreover be wiser than they. For this fine power of theirs usually ceases with them where art ceases and life begins; *we*, however, want to be the poets of our life, and first of all in the smallest and most commonplace matters.

300.

Prelude to Science.—Do you believe then that the sciences would have arisen and grown up if the sorcerers, alchemists, astrologers and witches had not been their forerunners; those who, with their promisings and foreshadowings, had first to create a thirst, a hunger, and a taste for *hidden and forbidden* powers? Yea, that infinitely more had to be *promised* than could ever be fulfilled, in order that something might be fulfilled in the domain of knowledge? Perhaps the whole of *religion*, also, may appear to some distant age as an exercise and a prelude, in like manner as the prelude and preparation of science here exhibit themselves, though *not* at all practised and regarded as such. Perhaps religion may have been the peculiar means for enabling individual men to enjoy but once the entire self-satisfaction of a God and all his self-redeeming power. Indeed!—one may ask—would man have learned at all to get on the tracks of hunger and thirst for *himself*, and to extract satiety and fullness out of *himself*, without that religious schooling and preliminary history? Had Prometheus first to *fancy* that he had *stolen* the light, and that he did penance for the theft—in order finally to discover that he had created the light, *in that he had longed for the light*, and that not only man, but also *God* had been the work of *his* hands and the clay in his hands? All mere creations of the creator?—just as the illusion, the theft, the Caucasus, the vulture, and the whole tragic Prometheia of all thinkers!

301.

Illusion of the Contemplative.—Higher men are distinguished from lower, by seeing and hearing immensely more, and in a thoughtful manner—and it is precisely this that distinguishes man from the animal, and the higher animal from the lower. The world always becomes fuller for him who grows up into the full stature of humanity; there are always more interesting fishing-hooks, thrown out to him; the number of his stimuli is continually on the increase, and similarly the varieties of his pleasure and pain,—the higher man becomes always at the same time happier and unhappier. An *illusion*, however, is his constant accompaniment all along: he thinks he is placed as a *spectator* and *auditor* before the great pantomime and concert of life; he calls his nature a *contemplative nature*, and thereby overlooks the fact that he himself is also a real creator, and continuous poet of life,—that he no doubt differs greatly from the *actor* in this drama, the so-called practical man, but differs still more from a mere onlooker or spectator *before* the stage. There is certainly *vis contemplativa*, and re-examination of his work peculiar to him as poet, but at the same time, and first and foremost, he has the *vis creativa*, which the practical man or doer *lacks*, whatever appearance and current belief may say to the contrary. It is we, we who think and feel, that actually and unceasingly *make* something which does not yet exist: the whole eternally increasing world of valuations, colors, weights, perspectives, gradations, affirmations and negations. This composition of ours is continually learnt, practised, and translated into flesh and actuality, and even into the commonplace, by the so-called practical men (our actors, as we have said). Whatever has *value* in the present world, has it not in itself, by its nature,—nature is always worthless:—but a value was once given to it, bestowed upon it, and it was *we* who gave and bestowed! We only have created the world *which is of any account to man*!—But it is precisely this knowledge that we lack, and when we get hold of it for a moment we have forgotten it the next: we misunderstand our highest power, we contemplative men, and estimate ourselves at too low a rate,—we are neither as *proud nor as happy* as we might be.

302.

The Danger of the Happiest Ones.—To have fine senses and a fine taste; to be accustomed to the select and the intellectually best as our proper and readiest fare; to be blessed with a strong, bold, and daring soul; to go through life with a quiet eye and a firm step, ever ready for the worst as for a festival, and full of longing for undiscovered worlds and seas, men and Gods; to listen to all joyous music, as if there, perhaps, brave men, soldiers and seafarers, took a brief repose and enjoyment, and in the profoundest pleasure of the moment were overcome with tears and the whole purple melancholy of happiness: who would not like all this to be *his* possession, his condition! It was the *happiness of Homer*! The condition of him who invented the Gods for the Greeks,—nay, who invented *his* Gods for himself! But let us not conceal the fact that with this happiness of Homer in one's soul, one is more liable to suffering than any other creature under the sun! And only at this price do we purchase the most precious pearl that the waves of existence have hitherto washed ashore! As its possessor one always becomes more sensitive to pain, and at last too sensitive: a little displeasure and loathing sufficed in the end to make Homer disgusted with life. He was unable to solve a foolish little riddle which some young fishers proposed to him! Yes, the little riddles are the dangers of the happiest ones!

FRANZ KAFKA
THE METAMORPHOSIS

trans. Ian Johnston

Marx and Engels may have identified the withering nature of life in a capitalist, bureaucratic society, but Kafka's The Metamorphosis *conveys the full weight of its burden. It is a piece of art so brilliantly accomplished that its ostensibly outlandish premise—a man wakes up as an insect—resonates with anyone who has spent their lives hunched over a desk, involved in some triviality in order to meet their most basic responsibilities. In Gregor's glib optimism, prioritizing of the mundane, emphasis on keeping up appearances, and pushing what is essential off to a tomorrow he is unlikely to ever inhabit, we feel the abject state the world will consign us to in order to achieve its own designs.*

One morning, as Gregor Samsa was waking up from anxious dreams, he discovered that in bed he had been changed into a monstrous verminous bug. He lay on his armor-hard back and saw, as he lifted his head up a little, his brown, arched abdomen divided up into rigid bow-like sections. From this height the blanket, just about ready to slide off completely, could hardly stay in place. His numerous legs, pitifully thin in comparison to the rest of his circumference, flickered helplessly before his eyes.

"What's happened to me," he thought. It was no dream. His room, a proper room for a human being, only somewhat too small, lay quietly between the four well-known walls. Above the table, on which an unpacked collection of sample cloth goods was spread out—Samsa was a traveling salesman—hung the picture which he had cut out of an illustrated magazine a little while ago and set in a pretty gilt frame. It was a picture of a woman with a fur hat and a fur boa. She sat erect there, lifting up in the direction of the viewer a solid fur muff into which her entire forearm had disappeared.

Gregor's glance then turned to the window. The dreary weather—the rain drops were falling audibly down on the metal window ledge—made him quite melancholy. "Why don't I keep sleeping for a little while longer and forget all this foolishness," he thought. But this was entirely impractical, for he was used to sleeping on his right side, and in his present state he couldn't get himself into this position. No matter how hard he threw himself onto his right side, he always rolled again onto his back. He must have tried it a hundred times, closing his eyes so that he would not have to see the wriggling legs, and gave up only when he began to feel a light, dull pain in his side which he had never felt before.

"O God," he thought, "what a demanding job I've chosen! Day in, day out, on the road. The stresses of selling are much greater than the work going on at head office, and, in addition to that, I have to cope with the problems of traveling, the worries about train connections, irregular bad food, temporary and constantly changing human relationships, which never come from the heart. To hell with it all!" He felt a slight itching on the top of his abdomen. He slowly pushed himself on his back closer to the bed post so that he could lift his head more easily, found the itchy part, which was entirely covered with small white spots—he did not know what to make of them and wanted to feel the place with a leg. But he retracted it immediately, for the contact felt like a cold shower all over him.

He slid back again into his earlier position. "This getting up early," he thought, "makes a man quite idiotic. A man must have his sleep. Other traveling salesmen live like harem wo-men. For instance, when I come back to the inn during the course of the morning to write up the necessary orders, these gentlemen are just sitting down to breakfast. If I were to try that with my boss, I'd be thrown out on the spot. Still, who knows whether that mightn't be really good for me? If I didn't hold back for my parents' sake, I'd have quit ages ago. I would've gone to the boss and told him just what I think from the bottom of my heart. He would've fallen right off his desk! How weird it is to sit up at that desk and talk down to the employee from way up there. The boss has trouble hearing, so the employee has to step up quite close to him. Anyway, I haven't completely given up that hope yet. Once I've got together the money to pay off my parents' debt to him—that should take another five or six years—I'll do it for sure. Then I'll make the big break. In any case, right now I have to get up. My train leaves at five o'clock."

He looked over at the alarm clock ticking away by the chest of drawers. "Good God!" he thought. It was half past six, and the hands were going quietly on. It was past the half hour, already nearly quarter to. Could the alarm have failed to ring? One saw from the bed that it was properly set for four o'clock. Certainly it had rung. Yes, but was it possible to sleep through that noise which made the furniture shake? Now, it's true he'd not slept quietly, but evidently he'd slept all the more deeply. Still, what should he do now? The next train left at seven o'clock. To catch that one, he would have to go in a mad rush. The sample collection wasn't packed up yet, and he really didn't feel particularly fresh and active. And even if he caught the train, there was no avoiding a blow-up with the boss, because the firm's errand boy would've waited for the five o'clock train and reported the news of his absence long ago. He was the boss's minion, without backbone or intelligence. Well then, what if he reported in sick? But that would be extremely embarrassing and suspicious, because during his five years' service Gregor hadn't been sick even once. The boss would certainly come with the doctor from the health insurance company and would reproach his parents for their lazy son and cut short all objections with the insurance doctor's comments; for him everyone was completely healthy but really lazy about work. And besides, would the doctor in this case be totally wrong? Apart from a really excessive drowsiness after the long sleep, Gregor in fact felt quite well and even had a really strong appetite.

As he was thinking all this over in the greatest haste, without being able to make the decision to get out of bed—the alarm clock was indicating exactly quarter to seven—there was a cautious knock on the door by the head of the bed.

"Gregor," a voice called—it was his mother!— "it's quarter to seven. Don't you want to be on your way?" The soft voice! Gregor was startled when he heard his voice answering. It was clearly and unmistakably his earlier voice, but in it was intermingled, as if from below, an irrepressibly painful squeaking, which left the words positively distinct only in the first moment and distorted them in the reverberation, so that one didn't know if one had heard correctly. Gregor wanted to answer in detail and explain everything, but in these circumstances he confined himself to saying, "Yes, yes, thank you mother. I'm getting up right away." Because of the wooden door the change in Gregor's voice was not really noticeable outside, so his mother calmed down with this explanation and shuffled off. However, as a result of the short conversation, the other family members became aware that Gregor was unexpectedly still at home, and already his father was knocking on one side door, weakly but with his fist. "Gregor, Gregor," he called out, "what's going on?" And, after a short while, he urged him on again in a deeper voice: "Gregor!" Gregor!" At the other side door, however, his sister knocked lightly. "Gregor? Are you all right? Do you need anything?" Gregor directed answers in both directions, "I'll be ready right away." He made an effort with the most careful articulation and by inserting long pauses between the individual words to remove everything remarkable from his voice. His father turned back to his breakfast. However, the sister whispered, "Gregor, open the door—I beg you." Gregor had no intention of opening the door, but congratulated himself on his precaution, acquired from traveling, of locking all doors during the night, even at home.

First he wanted to stand up quietly and undisturbed, get dressed, above all have breakfast, and only then consider further action, for—he noticed this clearly—by thinking things over in bed he would not reach a reasonable conclusion. He remembered that he had already often felt a light pain or other in bed, perhaps the result of an awkward lying position, which later turned out to be purely imaginary when he stood up, and he was eager to see how his present fantasies would gradually dissipate. That the change in his voice was nothing other than the onset of a real chill, an occupational illness of commercial travelers, of that he had not the slightest doubt.

ALBERT EINSTEIN
RELATIVITY: THE SPECIAL & THE GENERAL THEORY

trans. Robert W. Lawson

A sign that the endeavor initiated by the Ancient Greeks has tunneled all the way through to the other side. That unflagging quest for the truth resolves itself in Einstein's discovery that what we perceive as being "true" is always contingent. Euclid's precepts are incontrovertible—so long as they are viewed within that framework. As Einstein expands to what is actually universal, we see that the only absolute informing our vision is that where we happen to be positioned is what shapes our experience. Suddenly, the target is in perpetual motion, at light speed. Depending on where you stand, humanity has either been set free, or adrift.

In your schooldays most of you who read this book made acquaintance with the noble building of Euclid's geometry, and you remember—perhaps with more respect than love—the magnificent structure, on the lofty staircase of which you were chased about for uncounted hours by conscientious teachers. By reason of our past experience, you would certainly regard everyone with disdain who should pronounce even the most out-of-the-way proposition of this science to be untrue. But perhaps this feeling of proud certainty would leave you immediately if some one were to ask you: "What, then, do you mean by the assertion that these propositions are true?" Let us proceed to give this question a little consideration.

Geometry sets out from certain conceptions such as "plane," "point," and "straight line," with which we are able to associate more or less definite ideas, and from certain simple propositions (axioms) which, in virtue of these ideas, we are inclined to accept as "true." Then, on the basis of a logical process, the justification of which we feel ourselves compelled to admit, all remaining propositions are shown to follow from those axioms, *i.e.* they are proven. A proposition is then correct ("true") when it has been derived in the recognized manner from the axioms. The question of "truth" of the individual geometrical propositions is thus reduced to one of the "truth" of the axioms. Now it has long been known that the last question is not only unanswerable by the methods of geometry, but that it is in itself entirely without meaning. We cannot ask whether it is true that only one straight line goes through two points. We can only say that Euclidean geometry deals with things called "straight lines," to each of which is ascribed the property of being uniquely determined by two points situated on it. The concept "true" does not tally with the assertions of pure geometry, because by the word "true" we are eventually in the habit of designating always the correspondence with a "real" object; geometry, however, is not concerned with the relation of the ideas involved in it to objects of experience, but only with the logical connection of these ideas among themselves.

It is not difficult to understand why, in spite of this, we feel constrained to call the propositions of geometry "true." Geometrical ideas correspond to more or less exact objects in nature, and these last are undoubtedly the exclusive cause of the genesis of those ideas. Geometry ought to refrain from such a course, in order to give to its structure the largest possible logical unity. The practice, for example, of seeing in a "distance" two marked positions on a practically rigid body is something which is lodged deeply in our habit of thought. We are accustomed further to regard three points as being situated on a straight line, if their apparent positions can be made to coincide for observation with one eye, under suitable choice of our place of observation.

If, in pursuance of our habit of thought, we now supplement the propositions of Euclidean geometry by the single proposition that two points on a practically rigid body always correspond to the same distance (line-interval), independently of any changes in position to which we may subject the body, the propositions of Euclidean geometry then resolve themselves into propositions on the possible relative position of practically rigid bodies. Geometry which has been supplemented in this way is then to be treated as a branch of physics. We can now legitimately ask as to the "truth" of geometrical propositions interpreted in this way, since we are justified in asking whether these propositions are satisfied for those real things we have associated with the geometrical ideas. In less exact terms we can express this by saying that by the "truth" of a geometrical proposition in this sense we understand its validity for a construction with rule and compasses.

Of course the conviction of the "truth" of geometrical propositions in this sense is founded exclusively on rather incomplete experience. For the present we shall assume the "truth" of the geometrical propositions, then at a later stage (in the general theory of relativity) we shall see that this "truth" is limited, and we shall consider the extent of its limitation.

ABOUT THE EDITOR

Matthew Doucet is a writer and editor who lives in the foothills of New Hampshire's White Mountains. He spends his time trawling the internet for music and arguing with friends about things they don't know all that much about. He is the author of two other entries in the Curio Series, *How to Talk Like You Know What You're Talking About* and *You've Never Heard Your Favorite Song*.

DISTILLED IDEAS
FOR CURIOUS MINDS

Curated to be useful, entertaining, and informative, Curios range from cultural appraisals to culinary guides, packing plenty of punch no matter the subject.

NO. 1

THE AVOCADO TOAST MANIFESTO
by ABIGAIL F. BROWN

NO. 2

HOW TO TALK LIKE YOU KNOW WHAT
YOU'RE TALKING ABOUT
by MATTHEW DOUCET

NO. 3

THE ULTIMATE EXCUSES HANDBOOK
by LOU HARRY & JULIA SPALDING

ABOUT CIDER MILL PRESS
BOOK PUBLISHERS

Good ideas ripen with time. From seed to harvest, Cider Mill Press brings fine reading, information, and entertainment together between the covers of its creatively crafted books. Our Cider Mill bears fruit twice a year, publishing a new crop of titles each spring and fall.

CIDER MILL PRESS

BOOK PUBLISHERS

"Where Good Books Are Ready for Press"

Visit us online at
www.cidermillpress.com
or write to us at
PO Box 454
12 Spring St.
Kennebunkport, Maine 04046